DAVID DALE of NEW LANARK

DAVID DALE of NEW LANARK

A Bright Luminary to Scotland

David J McLaren

Caring Books

© David J McLaren 1999

Printed in 1999 by
Caring Books, PO Box 1565,
Glasgow, G46 6SX

Printed and bound in Great Britain
by Bell & Bain Ltd.

British Library in Cataloguing Publication Data.

David McLaren asserts the moral right
to be identified as the author of this work.

ISBN 0-9523649-3-X

To Kirsty

ACKNOWLEDGMENTS

Thanks to the Mitchell Library, Glasgow, Glasgow University Library and the Strathclyde Regional Archives Department for permission to reproduce pictorial material.

Thanks also to the New Lanark Conservation Trust for permission to reproduce the cover illustration, which is a view of New Lanark circa 1818 by John Winning.

CONTENTS

"A BRIGHT LUMINARY TO SCOTLAND"[1]

When I first conceived of this research exercise, it was in terms of New Lanark and New Lanark alone. This was for the simple reason that I had previously done some minor research on Robert Owen's work with the School and New Institution there and had been impressed, not only with his advanced methods of teaching, but also with his attempts to improve the quality of life of the New Lanark villagers. Like many people (and many textbooks) I had regarded David Dale as rather a minor figure in the history of New Lanark — someone worthy of a mention but only in relation to Owen. It soon became obvious, however, that the mills at New Lanark had been in operation for some thirteen years before Owen took them over and "improved" them. This then made me wonder what it was that Owen had "improved" upon, and thus I had to look at Dale's involvement at New Lanark.

It then became clear that the man responsible for New Lanark was a man worthy of closer study in his own right. It also became clear that I was faced with what looked like a contradiction. On the one hand, Robert Owen's uncomplimentary description of Dale and New Lanark in *A New View of Society* contrasted sharply with the scraps of information I was able to gather on Dale, almost all of which praised him to the skies. On the other hand, given that Owen was prone to exaggeration and immodesty, it was quite possible that Owen had exaggerated the picture of Dale in order that Owen's own substantial achievement would seem all the more praiseworthy, and I set about looking for a "Life" of Dale to set the record straight.

Unfortunately, such a "Life" does not exist, as far as I know. Certainly, there are one or two potted histories, but these are often brief and tend to dwell on the anecdotal and apoc-

1 This title was given to Dale by the minister of the Parish of Kilmadock or Doune. *Old Statistical Account, Vol. XX, 1798.*

ryphal. The only solution was to attempt one myself, based, as far as possible, on the facts that I could gather. This proved no easy task, given the dearth of information, Dale's busy life, and the fact that he never appeared in print himself.

This biography looks in some detail at Dale's many and varied business interests in an attempt to get a clear picture of this man who seems so neglected by historians in general and educational historians in particular. I believe this neglect is quite unjustified: to describe him merely as a "merchant" or "founder of New Lanark" as so many people do, is tantamount to saying that Adam Smith was a teacher or John Knox a minister.

Any account of Dale's life must take into account the business side, the educational side, the philanthropic side and the religious side if any overall balanced impression is to be gained. The chapter headings reflect this, but any one chapter cannot be read in isolation since Dale was *all* of these things: businessman, educator, philanthropist and evangelist throughout his life.

Inevitably, perhaps, New Lanark, as his single greatest triumph (both in terms of his business career and his provision of schooling) is discussed more than some of his other ventures, and this is only right and proper. New Lanark, however, did not just "happen" and must be seen in the context of Dale's whole life and times, not just as a preface to Robert Owen's work. When Owen married into the Dale family, he inherited not only a factory with a school, but a tradition of concern for the employees and their children — call it 'philanthropy' if you will — which was evident throughout Dale's life.

Thus it is precisely because Dale was all of the things mentioned above that it is necessary to set him in the context of each of these headings. It is also necessary on occasions to take time to set particular elements of "business", "education" and so on in their historical context, i.e. where necessary to explain the origins of a particular partnership of Dale's or a particular institution with which he was associated. The result is, I hope, a balanced view of David Dale which credits him with more than just founding New Lanark.

THE EARLY YEARS

David Dale's origin was extremely inauspicious. Born the son of William Dale, a grocer and general dealer in Stewarton, Ayrshire, on 6th January 1739, his first job was as a "herd laddie" in the village. Nothing is known of his brother Hugh, and very little of his father, except that he married again in later life and had another son, James, who also became a merchant in Glasgow [1] and was joint manager of the New Lanark Mills for a number of years.

The conditions in Ayrshire at the time of David Dale's birth seem to have been little influenced by the "improving" climate of the eighteenth century.

"The farmhouses," wrote the Chancellor of the Burgh of Prestwick, "were mere hovels, moated with clay and having an open fireplace in the midst of the floor ... the manure heap at the door ... no straw yards— hardly a potato or any other esculent root; no garden vegetables except a few Scotch kail which, with milk and oatmeal, formed the principal diet of the people." [2]

He added:

"There were no manufactures in the country, ex- cepting bonnets at Stewarton and a growing trade in carpets at Kilmarnock. Exports and imports at the harbours of Ayr, Irvine and Saltcoats were very trifling." [3]

From Stewarton, Dale went to Paisley to serve a weaving apprenticeship (i.e. hand weaving which involved passing the iron shuttle from hand to hand). At this early period in his life, dates are difficult to ascertain. Certainly it is known that he arrived in

Glasgow at the age of twenty-four, but from his childhood up until his arrival in Glasgow, no dates seem to be available. In the 1750's silk gauze manufacture was booming in Paisley, and later in the decade, Paisley was competing in the prestigious fashion market with the French. A combination of circumstances seems to have made Paisley the centre of a particularly lucrative market at this time. According to Murray,[4] cheap labour and what he calls "local skills" (presumably a tradition of domestic weaving which still existed in Paisley as late as 1838)[5] attracted the manufacturers. Added to this must be the proximity of water and the damp climate. By 1784, ten thousand people were employed in the silk gauze line, half of whom were weavers. (Silk of course declined as the cotton and linen markets expanded, but given the above conditions, it seems that the weavers could adapt and transfer their skills to cotton.)

Assuming, then, that Dale arrived in Paisley some time during the 1750's,[6] he almost certainly followed the pattern of apprenticeship of the time, i.e. of hand-loom weaving done at home, or at most in a shed where local weavers would gather to work. These sheds were of course a precursor of the 'factory' except that in these early 'factories' there were no set hours of work or standards of work to be achieved. The orders and raw materials came from an agent who would have someone deliver them, and terms were agreed on each order. The weaver(s) then got to work and the finished product was uplifted. If it was a big order, of course, many weavers would be involved, and in the early days this meant a lot of foot slogging on the part of the agent or his assistant, as the weavers were still very much home-based. It also meant different standards of work from different weavers and also, on occasions, different rates for the job.

Dale's apprenticeship appears to have been with these home-based weavers in Paisley. It is unclear at what point he left there, but again, according to the *Dictionary of Eminent Scotsmen*, he moved to Hamilton because he "disliked the sedentary occupation". It would seem that he was in pursuit of more action, which suggests that the various accounts of Dale tramping the

countryside delivering material and picking up completed mer-
chandise apply to the period *after* his Paisley apprenticeship, i.e.
during his time as a journeyman in Hamilton and Cambuslang. [7]

Very little seems to be known of this period in Hamilton
and Cambuslang, except that he was probably employed tramping
the countryside in this way. It is possible, however, that the
Cambuslang period may have seen him in some kind of promoted
position as a clerk, which would explain his move to Glasgow as a
clerk. I have been unable to find any evidence for this, and even
the date of his removal to Glasgow is unclear.

He worked as a clerk to a silk mercer for a while. Presumably his apprenticeship with the hand-loom silk weavers in Paisley
and his experience in Hamilton and Cambuslang would help to
elevate him to this position of clerk, not to mention his friends in
the College church at the time. Indeed, after this time as a clerk
in Glasgow, it is noted that "With the assistance of friends he
commenced business on his own account in the linen yarn trade",[8]
which suggests that Dale, quite naturally, used the experience he
had gained in the trade and the Church to raise capital for this
important new venture.

Archibald Paterson, one of Dale's church friends and a well-
known candlemaker in the city, became Dale's partner in the one-
room shop in Hopkirk's Land on the east side of the High Street.
This was in 1763 and the shop was five doors from Glasgow Cross
in the heart of commercial Glasgow. At least one writer [9] is con-
vinced that Paterson provided the money for the venture, and this
is probably true, since, as will be seen later, Paterson seems to
have been a sleeping partner in the business. Also, Paterson would
appear to have been a man of some wealth, since he was able to
finance the erection of a meeting house a year or so later. (See
Chapter 6.) However, this is not to suggest that Paterson was the
only person to support the venture financially; merely that his
name was more prominent than anyone else's.

It is important at this point to stress the fundamental
change in the lifestyle of David Dale, even at this early stage in
his career. By that I do not mean that at the age of twenty-four

he suddenly found himself a rich man and lived the rest of his life in luxury. Dale did enjoy great prosperity and comfortable surroundings, but this was only a gradual process. The point is that Dale's life changed from weaver to merchant or trader with a base and capital from which to work: he became a business-man. Exactly why he became a businessman can only be hinted at, but there are a number of possible reasons. His father, rather than see his son stay in Stewarton, sent him to learn a trade in Paisley, the heart of the Scottish weaving industry. From here, Dale was on his own, but was astute enough to realise that money could be made in buying, manufacturing and selling material. This, combined with an almost Calvinistic attitude towards work (see Chapter 6) and a genuine talent for making money, ensured Dale's success as an entrepreneur.

The Hopkirk's Land shop was, by any standards, a modest affair. The room had an annual rent of £5, yet, small as it was, Dale sub-let half of it to a watchmaker to ease the payment of rent, and in fact continued to be associated with it after 1783 when it became the first Glasgow branch of the Royal Bank of Scotland. Dale and Paterson used the shop for selling imported French yarns, but Paterson took no share in the management of the company, particularly when it started to import linen yarns from Flanders and Holland.[10] However, it was probably Pater-son's name which was used for trading in the first few years because Dale's name does not appear until 1769 as a Burgher and Member of the Guild Brethren.[11] Although, strictly speaking, this gave Dale the title of "merchant", the fee which he paid really only gave him the right to function as a trader in the city, and all who were in business had to do likewise. A further annual fee was required by the Merchants' House before any merchant could have any voting rights or be eligible for election to office within the house. It was a further eighteen years before Dale became a full Matriculated member of the Merchants' House, by which time he had become well-known in the city. Nevertheless, it is important to note that after six years in the Hopkirk's Land shop he was able to use his own name to trade in Glasgow. He had completed the transition from weaver to entrepreneur. As if to seal this transition, he made a "good" marriage. In 1777 he married Ann Caroline Campbell, daughter of one of the Edinburgh Directors of the Royal Bank, and a member of a family which Robert Owen was to find very useful later on when he required capital to keep New Lanark functioning.

References and Notes

1   *The Biographical Dictionary of Eminent Scotsmen*, London, Blackie, 1874.
.2   G. Stewart, *Curiosities of Glasgow Citizenship*, Glasgow, Maclehose, 1881, pp. 45-7.
3   Ibid. p. 45-7.
4   N. Murray, *Scottish Handloom Weavers 1790-1850: A Social History*, Edinburgh, J. Donald, 1978, Ch. 1.
5   Ibid. p. 13.
6   I cannot verify this but the *Dictionary of Eminent Scotsmen* notes that at that time, weaving was "the most lucrative trade in the country", which suggests that the period referred to is around 1750-60, since this was the beginning of the 'boom' time in weaving. See Reference 2, p. 422.
7   G. Stewart, *Curiosities* . . . op. cit., pp. 45-7.
8   *Biographical Dictionary*, op. cit.

9   Senex (R. Reid), *Glasgow Past and Present*, Glasgow, 1884, Vol. 3, p. 372.

10 See also N. Munro, *The History of the Royal Bank 1727-1927*, Edinburgh, Clark, 1928, p. 157.

11 J.R. Anderson (Ed.), *The Burgesses and Guild Brethren of Glasgow*, Scottish Records Society, Vol 2.

PARTNERSHIPS IN PROSPERITY

On 24th May 1782, the following advertisement appeared in the *Glasgow Journal*:

> "The partnership between Archibald Paterson and David Dale carried on under the firm of David Dale & Co. is dissolved . . . David Dale continues to carry on the same business on his own account."

Paterson is reported in Senex (R. Reid)[1] as feeling snubbed by this for some time but apparently forgave Dale, owing to the fact that by this time they had been members of the same church for a number of years. Exactly why Dale dissolved the partnership is unclear, but there are a number of possibilities. Firstly, as I have suggested, Paterson was really a sleeping partner and had been from the start. Secondly, Dale had been trading under his own name for eleven years and profits must have been substantial. (Even if the profits were not massive his name was well enough known to make credit a relatively simple matter.) Thirdly, his marriage to Ann Caroline (or Carolina as he called her) may have brought him some extra money to add to his profits, because in the same year he had the mansion in Charlotte Street built at a cost of £6,000.[1b] Finally, it is quite possible that Dale knew of the Royal Bank appointment to come in the following year because of his father-in-law's position of Director, and may have wished Paterson out of the way to make room, as it were, for the bank. (The watchmaker's services were also dispensed with.) The two latter suggestions are supported by the *Dictionary of Eminent Scotsmen* and Andrew Liddell, author of the only genuine attempt at a biography of Dale:

> "There is reason to suppose that her father's con-

nection with the Royal Bank of Scotland as Director
led to Mr Dale's appointment as agent of that establishment in Glasgow and this increased his commercial
credit and command of capital." [2]

He was appointed agent along with one Robert Scott Mon-
crieff, a merchant in Edinburgh. This was the first time Dale and
Moncrieff met in business, but it was not the last. Moncrieff is
usually described as a merchant, but at the time of the move to
Glasgow, was the Deputy Receiver General and Receiver of the
Land Tax for Scotland. [2b]

In its assessment of the work of the first Glasgow branch of
the Royal Bank, *The Three Banks Review* notes that:

"When Robert Scott Moncrieff and David Dale were
appointed in 1783 they had to find caution to the
amount of £10,000 for their intromissions. In 1804
this Bond of £10,000 was discharged and delivered to
them, the Directors expressing the 'fullest conviction'
that in every respect they (Dale and Moncrieff) had
conducted the business entrusted to them 'with ability
as well as the strictest integrity'." [3]

In other words, they borrowed £10,000 from businessmen
(mostly on the east coast of Scotland) as a form of 'security' in
return for permission to handle other people's money on the
Bank's behalf (although the firm traded under the name of Scott
Moncrieff and Dale). [4] Hence the Directors would pay back this
sum when they felt the bank was suitably established and successful.

Successful it apparently was. It became the centre of a
great deal of business for the Royal Bank, and within fifty years
the Glasgow branch was doing more business than any other
individual office in Scotland or outside London. [5] This was
despite much competition from the other banks which established branches in Glasgow during the 1780's, indicating the city's

growing importance as a business centre. For example, this period saw in Glasgow the establishment of The Ship Bank, The Glasgow Arms Bank, The Thistle Bank, Merchant Banking Co., and "at least half a dozen like concerns originating from Stirling, Greenock, Falkirk, Paisley, Dundee and Renfrewshire".[6]

The Glasgow branch was established "for discounting bills . . . on London and Edinburgh and circulating their notes on Glasgow and the neighbourhood."[7]   These were Bills of Exchange, which were thought to be the quickest and most convenient way of financing the movement of goods. By 1793, Discounts of the Glasgow branch totalled £792,000 and by the end of the century had reached the £1m. mark.

According to *The Three Banks Review*:

> "Bills were discounted twice weekly on Tuesdays and Fridays but by 1800 anything from 200–400 were being discounted daily. Customers placed their bills a day or so before discounting in a wooden box with a slit which stood on the counter. At the close of business for the day, the bills were examined by the 'first accomptant' who, after due enquiry and with due reference to the agents, extracted those elegantly described as 'not convenient for discounting'. Those to be paid were marked with the appropriate rate of discount, then from 5–7% according to the type and tenor of the bill; the bills being collected by the customer in due course." [8]

The Bill of Exchange is a rather complicated piece of machinery which had its roots in medieval times, when it originally meant a written promise to pay a person in another town a sum of money. According to G. Parker in *The Emergence of Modern Finance in Europe 1500–1730*,"Every bill of exchange involved a short term loan, possibly at interest." [9] This type of credit transfer would mean that the bank would lend Merchant A the money to pay Merchant B. Merchant A would be charged in-

terest on this loan and all he had to do was write out a simple
note, promising to pay Merchant B the money (by credit transfer)
by a certain date. If Merchant B wanted his money before that
date, the bank gave him it, less a 'discount' of 5–7%. Merchant B
could, of course, account for this loss by charging Merchant A a
higher price for the goods in the first place. Thus the bills mentioned above which were "not convenient for discounting" would
be those which were considered to be a bad risk and which could
not be paid before the agreed date.

The loans for these bills were normally short-term loans, i.e.
of a few weeks, but there is evidence[10] that Dale granted long-
term loans with up to twelve months to pay. This might explain
why Dale and Moncrieff had to pay such a large sum to the Royal
Bank and it helps to explain why they had to raise over £111,000
capital to start the finance business in the first place.[11]

It must be borne in mind that Dale was now both merchant
and banker and in a sense got the best of both worlds. That is, he
continued in the textile business, buying and selling yarn (and a
new venture in dyeing) which meant that profit was still available
to him, and if his deal with another merchant was on a large scale,
that merchant could always borrow money from the Royal Bank,
of which Dale just happened to be an agent. Dale's bargaining
power in a business venture must have been greatly enhanced
when he became an agent for the bank. If the other merchant
wanted time to pay the bill, then that was a possibility too.

This seems a rather leisurely approach to banking, and
indeed Munro, in his *History of the Royal Bank*[12], refers to it
as "a leisure-hour recreation, like the game of golf". Certainly,
Dale's partner had had experience of money matters in Edinburgh
as Deputy Receiver General and Receiver of the Land Tax for
Scotland, and Checkland's work on the Moncrieff letters[13]
seems to bear out the fact that Moncrieff was doing most of the
banking work — certainly towards the end of Dale's association
with the bank. (Dale handed over to Mr John More in 1800.)
While I would not go so far as to refer to it as a "leisure-hour recreation", I would argue that, given Dale's many ventures in the

world of business during the 1790's, he was well aware of the influence he had as an agent and spent a lot of time away from the shop in Hopkirk's Land. Even in the early days of his banking career he must have realised that the position of agent could do him nothing but good. His social status in the city was already growing — (he had helped found the first Chamber of Commerce in 1783 and served six years as a Director and two as Chairman) — and the appointment as agent would enhance this status. He would not only be able to meet other businessmen, but would be in a position to help them in money matters, and he could use the bank's money to finance his own ventures in the future, as suggested by S.G. Checkland in his *History* of Scottish banking:

> "As early as 1788 the Royal Bank had made large advances to Glasgow mill owners and was obliged to sustain them in the crisis of that year. It is tantalising that we know so little of how David Dale financed his own interest in cotton spinning." [14]

In other words, from 1783 onwards, Dale was no longer just a wealthy merchant, but one who was to have access to power and influence in the city. It is significant that Dale's business ventures really started to take off during the early 1780's.

One of the first of these ventures, and the one which was to bring the name of David Dale to the attention of the world, was New Lanark. Dale met Richard Arkwright, his original partner in the venture, at a public dinner in Glasgow attended by bankers, merchants and manufacturers.[15] Arkwright had apparently got in touch with "The Patriot of the North", Mr George Dempster, (later to be associated with Dale at Spinningdale), and both came to the dinner. Dale took Arkwright with him on the following day to view the proposed site of the mills — the first big spinning enterprise in Scotland, though in fact other cotton mills had been established in Scotland prior to this date: at Penicuik in 1778; Neilston (Gateside Mill) in 1780; Johnstone (Old End Mill) in 1782 and the Deanston and Stanley Mills in 1785.[16]

By the time Arkwright had arrived in Glasgow in 1783, he had achieved considerable fame (or notoriety in England) over his spinning frame and patents. Arkwright had patented a roller spinning machine in 1769 when he moved from Lancashire to Nottingham with his assistant, John Kay, a clockmaker. However, the idea of a rolling machine was not new. Baines, in *The History of the Cotton Manufacture*[17] argues that Lewis Paul had taken out a patent for a similar machine thirty-one years earlier. Also, it is argued that John Kay, when he constructed the machine from wood, was using a design stolen from Kay's original employer, Thomas Highs of Leigh. In any case, it is now widely accepted that even if Arkwright did use Highs' designs (and Highs never patented them) he improved them to such an extent that they hardly resembled the models of Highs, and Arkwright actually got his machine working, which was more than Highs ever did.

Arkwright's machine of 1769 is illustrated opposite. The principle is that cardings of cotton are drawn out by a number of pairs of rollers placed horizontally. The carding is fed between the first pair of rollers to compress it and draw it out and then it is fed through another pair of rollers which are revolving faster than the first pair. This draws out the sliver even further and makes it finer. The next pair of rollers are revolving even faster, and so the cotton becomes longer and finer as it passes through each pair of rollers. Finally, the sliver is twisted and wound on to a bobbin, the whole process being water-powered.

In 1771, Arkwright entered into partnership with Jedediah Strutt of Derby to erect the Cromford Mill, and an enlarged version of the machine (which came to be known as the "water frame") was used there. This partnership lasted eleven years until Strutt continued on his own at Belper and Arkwright retained Cromford.

By this time, Hargreaves had invented his "spinning jenny" (also illustrated). Here, the spindles are in a vertical position and the cardings are clasped between two horizontal bars of wood while the cotton is drawn out, lengthened and spun into yarn. Hargreaves' machine made weft and Arkwright's made warp, so

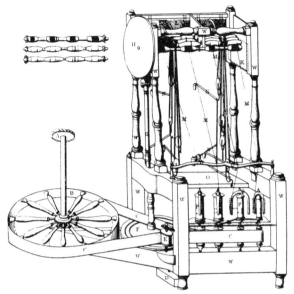

Sir Richard Arkwright's Spinning Machine. Patent 1769

Hargreaves' Spinning Jenny

the machines were not in conflict with each other. However, in
the 1770's these machines were felt by many workers in the north
of England to be a threat to jobs and there were riots during this
period. (Crompton's Mule Jenny, invented in 1779, which was a
combination of water frame and Spinning Jenny, only added to
the workers' fears.)

Arkwright, by this time a target for the rioters, further
aggravated the situation by alienating himself from his fellow
cotton spinners. This came about largely because of two patents
in 1775. The first of these was his carding patent where cotton
was carded by a series of comb-like instruments, but it may be
that Hargreaves was the original inventor of this machine[17], and
Lewis Paul had invented a machine for carding cotton using
rollers. Arkwright's second patent of that year was for a *series* of
machines – carding, drawing and roving (twisting). He claimed to
be the "first and sole inventor thereof".

Arkwright was already a prosperous man, but if he could
legally enforce his patents, he stood to make a fortune. (Indeed
he had already made money by selling grants of his patents.)
Naturally, the other cotton spinners stood to lose by this, and in
any case there was considerable doubt about the validity of his
patents. In a court action in 1781, the judgement went in favour
of Arkwright, which meant that some thirty thousand people
were technically breaking the law, and this number was increasing
because of the expansion in the cotton trade at that time. The
others retaliated and had the judgement reversed in the same year.
When Arkwright tried to consolidate the 1769 and 1775 patents,
he became one of the most unpopular men in England and again
lost the case.

By 1784, when he arrived in Glasgow, the other mill owners
were preparing the case for the final attempt to stop Arkwright
from gaining a monopoly. Thus it was that when he met Dale,
Arkwright was in the middle of litigation and probably open to
any business proposition which would get him out of the north
of England, particularly the Manchester area, since the mobs had
already made up their minds that he was guilty. Matthew Bolton

is reported as saying to Watt of Arkwright in 1781:

" . . . He swears he will take the cotton spinning abroad and that he will ruin those Manchester rascals he has been the making of . . . "[18]

Also, when in Glasgow, Arkwright is supposed to have remarked that he "would find a razor to shave Manchester."[19]

In this frame of mind, then, after the visit to New Lanark with Dale, Arkwright was "so satisfied that he voluntary offered to become a principal partner in the speculation."[20] Land was cleared and building immediately begun, but owing to the difficulty in excavating a rocky hill that interfered with the necessary water supply, spinning did not commence until March 1786.[21] The *Old Statistical Account for Scotland* bears this out.[22](This was a statistical account for each parish which was compiled in the 1790's.) Three months later, Dale had the first mill insured for £4,800: £2,000 for the mill buildings, £2,500 for the machinery and utensils and £300 for two houses. [23]

In the meantime, the court found against Arkwright in 1785, and it is significant that at this point the partnership between Dale and Arkwright was severed. Various sources[24] state that they split because of an argument over the position of the wooden belfry in the village, but this seems highly unlikely. More probable is that Dale wished to continue at New Lanark without the discredited Arkwright as a partner, since Arkwright's name could be prejudicial to trade, and managed to dispose of him in much the same way as he had disposed of Paterson in the High Street three years earlier, although not before he had availed himself of the opportunity of sending some of his mechanics to Cromford to be instructed in the operation of the machinery to be used at New Lanark. The most likely reason for the split is that when the partnership was formed, the case against Arkwright had not been heard, and so Dale could have been protecting his options. That is, if Arkwright had won the case, then thousands of spinners would have been breaking the law. By being in partnership with Arkwright, Dale could avoid this eventuality. He was not dependent on Arkwright for money [25], so when the decision went against Arkwright, there was no reason for Dale to be concerned about infringement of patent and the partnership was, strictly speaking, unnecessary. They parted company in 1785, although they were still in contact in 1788 regarding machinery.[26] Arkwright returned to England to run his mills at Cromford and Nottingham, was given a knighthood in 1786 after a loyal address to George III, and died in 1792, leaving nearly half a million pounds. Dale was now free to proceed at New Lanark.

The first mill, erected in 1785, was burned down in 1788. (Fire was always a problem in the early mills owing to the dust and the use of candles for lighting.) Dale kept his workforce fed and clothed and paid their wages while this mill was rebuilt, along with three others, and by 1791, 981 persons were employed in the mills. This increased to 1334 by November 1793. The total number of spindles in No. 1 and No. 2 mills was 10,500, but No. 3 had more because it was operated by water-powered 'jennies' patented by Dale's manager, Mr William Kelly. This new adaptation of the original machinery meant that an employee could operate twice as many spindles as before — benefiting both Dale and his workers.

New Lanark, of course, was to make Dale even more famous, not just because of its profits or because it was one of the first major mills in Scotland, but because of the conditions in which his employees lived, both his paid employees and his "apprentices". I shall return to this in a later chapter. Suffice it to say here that all these factors combined to make New Lanark a very famous institution before Owen took it over in 1799. If evidence of this is needed, one only has to look at the Visitors Book [27] starting in 1795 to see that _Dale's_ New Lanark had already become something of a showpiece.

As well as local businessmen and dignitaries such as Adam Bogle, Robert Tennant (with whom Dale was to invest in the mines at Barrowfield), James Gillespie, James Finlay, Archibald Paterson, Claud Alexander of Ballochmyle (his partner at Catrine),

James Watt, Charles MacIntosh and Scott Moncrieff, a wide variety of people from overseas visited New Lanark during the period 1795–1799. The Visitors Book contains the signatures of students, advocates, writers, Peers, ministers, soldiers and schoolmasters from such far-flung places as Norway, Jamaica, New York, Germany, Spain, India and Geneva. The total number of visitors per year was about 750, and it seems only fair to say that what has been called "Owen's New Lanark" in so many books and on so many television programmes ought really to be called *"Dale's New Lanark"*. Similarly, amongst all the names in the book, one, perhaps more than the others, stands out. On June 15th 1798, Robert Owen visited New Lanark and signed the Visitors Book. Referring to this in his *Life*, he described it as " . . . a primitive manufacturing Scotch village and four mills for spinning cotton." [28]

"Primitive" it may have been by modern standards, but it sufficiently interested Owen to induce him to return a year later in July 1799 with Messrs Atkinson and Barton from Manchester, with a view to purchase. And why not? It was already well-known and profitable, and the social and educational provisions which Owen was to expand were already in existence. (Despite Owen's constant efforts in his writings to minimise Dale's achievements.)

By the time Owen got to New Lanark, however, a great deal had happened to Dale and this has to be borne in mind in any discussion of New Lanark, since many textbooks see New Lanark as his only achievement. While it is true that the mills and village there brought him to the attention of the world, to see it as his only significant business venture is to deny Dale the success he achieved in other business ventures during the New Lanark period.

Before spinning had actually started at New Lanark, Dale was involved in 1785 with George MacIntosh (himself a factory owner concerned with manufacturing dyestuffs, and whose son' was later to give his name to a popular style of raincoat) and a M. Papillon from Rouen, in the creation of, according to *The Old Statistical Account:*

" . . . an extensive dyehouse in Dalmarnock . . .

where cotton is dyed real Turkey red, equal in beauty
and solidity to East India colours." [29]

"Turkey red" was so-called because Turkey cultivated the
madder plant from whose roots the dye was originally made. The
yarn had to go through some fourteen successive stages using
alkalis and a mixture of rancid olive oil, cow dung and soda, and
then had to be boiled in the dyebath with the madder, oxblood
and tannin. This process produced a yarn with a brilliant red
colour.

Papillon left a few years later and established his own
works, also in the parish, leaving Dale and MacIntosh to continue
on their own.

There is no record of any school (or any child employees)
at this factory, and there appear to be no records of Dale's involvement in an "inkle" (linen tape) factory around the same
time. [30] The Dalmarnock factory was sold to Henry Monteith in
1805. However, two points emerge from Dale's participation at
Dalmarnock. Firstly, the name George MacIntosh is associated
with Dale again at a later date in connection with Spinningdale.
Secondly, Dale's interest in dyeing, according to A. Cullen in his
book *Adventures in Socialism*, [31] led Dale to establish the
Blantyre cotton mill in 1787. This was sold to James Monteith in
1792 and Cullen argues that it was Monteith who provided the
schooling. However, I shall argue in a later chapter that it was
Dale who established the schooling for the children.

A clearer picture of Dale's involvement in cotton spinning
outside New Lanark can be seen in the partnership with Claud
Alexander of Ballochmyle in the establishement of the Catrine
Cotton Works in Ayrshire. These were built in 1787 (i.e. one year
after New Lanark started production). Some sources state 1786
as the date, but in a letter to Alexander dated 14th February
1787, Dale mentions that he has had an offer from a Mr Abercrombie to manage the mill in return for £250 per annum. Of
Abercrombie's terms, Dale says:

"I think them rather too high and we must therefore

look out for some other person unless he can be brought to more reasonable terms." [32]

The fact that they appear to be searching for a manager at this date suggests, perhaps, that the mill was not yet in operation and that construction (which may have begun in 1786) was still in progress.

Whatever the case, the mill was built in the centre of the village square. It had five storeys plus attics, and houses were built around the square. (See map on page 26.) Another mill was built in 1790 to house 76 spinning jennies and by 1793 the population had reached nearly 1,000. [33] By the time the Rev. Robert Steven came to write the return for *The Old Statistical Account* in 1796, 445 persons were employed in the twist mill, 118 of whom were under 12 years of age. A further 200 were employed in the "jeanie factory", 43 of whom were under 12 years of age – all from a population of 1,350 people. [34]

The "community" element in Catrine seems to have been strong and this was helped by Alexander's provision of an area of ground which he prepared for the villagers in order that they might plant potatoes for the winter. The villagers paid him a small sum and spent their hours after work in the fields:

"The dressing of the potato is the employment of both old and young on the summer evenings, after they are dismissed from the mills." [35]

The village also contained a corn mill, a brewery, and a loom for weaving. It was not, however, possible for just anyone to come to Catrine in the hope of employment:

"Certificates are required from the respective parishes in which they last resided." [36]

Those in the twist mill had to be particularly industrious because Mr Alexander

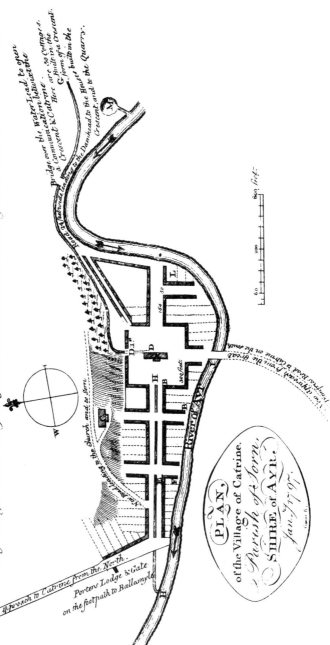

Engraved for the XX.th Vol. of Sir John Sinclair's Statistical Account of SCOTLAND. P.185.

PLAN,
of the Village of Catrine.
Parish of Sorn.
SHIRE of AYR.
Jan.ry 1795.

A, The twist-mill, in the centre of a square of 300 feet. The great wheel has a fall of 29½ feet.

B to B, The jeanie factory; the carding and roving in which is performed by the water after it comes from the twist mill, the lade from which is all arched.

C, The church.

DD, Is an aqueduct-bridge, which conveys the water from the hill to the top of the twist-mill wheel.

E, Is the corn-mill, and is also worked by the tail-water of the twist-mill.

F, Is a situation feued for a wauk or fulling mill.

From G to D 1/2, Is the water brought from the dam to the aqueduct-bridge.

H to H, Is the tail-water from the twist-mill; it is arched until it passes through the square, and then runs through the centre of the principal street, with bridges over it opposite to the three cross streets.

I, Is a proposed bridge over the river Ayr, to communicate with the Dumfries road.

L, A brewery.

M, A fine free-stone quarry.

N. B. The proprietor of the village of Catrine does not feu to the river side, but has reserved the ground along the river for a walk, 12 or 15 feet broad, for the health of the inhabitants, and which he is now facing with a stone and lime wall.

"... whilst he gives every encouragement to the
sober and industrious, he dismisses the riotous and
idle as unworthy to eat the company's bread."[36]

According to the minister, then, the village was thriving.
There was plenty of work, good wages, and the inhabitants were
well lodged, fed and clothed and the children went to a school.
(See Chapter 4.) Not surprisingly, it is Mr Alexander's name
which features strongly in the *Old Statistical Account*, since he
was the local landowner and farmed 100 acres of his own. Nevertheless, Dale was the other partner in this venture, and while
Alexander seems to have been the local 'boss', Dale certainly kept
in regular contact with him, as witnessed in Dale's letters to him
regarding the state of the market, the provision of equipment and
even of a fire engine and buckets.[37]

The illustration on page 29 shows the contents of a letter
from Dale to Alexander on 9th November 1789 with a list of the
selling prices of cotton twist (the higher the number the thicker
the yarn) and a note to the effect that 1576 spindles were in
operation in the daytime and 480 at night. In 1793 Dale wrote to
Alexander about their London agent, Mr Ingram, who had "transferred" some £6000 of the company's money into some other
venture. Fearing that this money was lost, Dale wrote:

"... This disappointment has much distraught me
and I much fear that I shall be obliged contrary both
to my inclination and intent to discharge a number of
work people on the weekly wages of Lanark and
Catrine."[37]

However, there is no evidence to show that he did lay off
any of his workers.

It seems that Dale was running the financial side of the
business and leaving the day to day management to Alexander
and his manager, in much the same way as he left the day to day
running of New Lanark to his own manager, Mr Kelly. The entire

Extract from an enclosure to a letter from Dale to Alexander dated 9th November 1789

9th Nov — 1576 Spindles going in the Day time
180 & during the Night

Pieces of the H[…] Berwit —
from 2d round 70lg

No.	£			£
18	1..13..4	5..7..	—	1..11.7½0
19	1..14.2	—		1.12.2¾
20	1..15..	—		1.12.11¼
21	1..15.10	—		1.13.8½
22	1..16.8	—		1.14.6½
23	1..17.6	—		1.15.5½
24	1..18.4	—		1.16.5¾
25	1..19.½	—		1.17.6½
26	2..2.1	—		1.18.3½
27	2..2.1	—		1.19.10½
28	2..3.4	—		2..1.1½
29	2..5.	—		2..2.6
30	2..9.8	—		2..3.11

works at Catrine were sold to James Finlay & Co. in 1801, and Archibald Buchanan took over as manager. He had been trained by Arkwright in the early days at Cromford and had managed the Buchanan family's cotton works at Ballindalloch and Deanston. Dale's partner in the Turkey red factory in Barrowfield, George MacIntosh, approached Dale in 1791 with the idea of establishing a factory in Dornoch in Sutherlandshire. In fact, he had approached Dale before, in 1783–4, to ask him to assist in saving the inhabitants of that region from famine. This Dale did, sending a ship from the south, loaded with white peas which were distributed free. Conditions had not improved much, and MacIntosh thought that a factory and community would help the situation. Thus it was that Dale went into partnership with MacIntosh, William Gillespie of Woodside and 18 others and established a small factory in a place called Spinningdale in the Parish of Creich. The name is reported as being Dale's own pun.[38] In fact, it is not a pun on Dale's name. The village had been referred to as Spinningdale (or variations of that name) for centuries. The company which ran the mill was known as the Balnoe company. One of the 18 partners was George Dempster, who, it will be remembered, had brought Arkwright to Glasgow in 1783 and was by 1791 the owner of the estate of Skibo in the Parish of Creich.

It would appear from a letter published in the *Scots Magazine* that Dale would have been happier if the Parish had involved itself in wool production rather than cotton, but, so great was his concern about the level of poverty and emigration in the Highlands, he agreed to proceed and any who wished to "emigrate" should come south, rather than cross the Atlantic. (Reference is also made to his famous "rescue" of 100 shipwrecked Highlanders.)

Glasgow, Oct. 20

Sir,

I am just favoured with your esteemed letter of the 19th current, and I have already done all that you suggest with respect to the Highland emigrants. So soon as I learned that they wished to continue in this country if they find employment to themselves and families, I sent two friends to Greenock, and invited old and young to come to this place, and I would give employment to them all. I have sent up in waggons a number of families to Lanark, and the rest are now in my house, waiting the return of the waggons to carry up the whole.

I have for some time past been devising every method I could think of to contribute my mite towards preventing these emigrations, which are no less hurtful to the poor people themselves than to this country; and I have been making attempts to introduce a branch of the cotton manufacture into the Highlands, which I find will soon spread, and employ a number of people; but I wish to see a plan executed that would enable the people of the Highlands and islands to work up their own wool; and I do not despair seeing an establishment of this kind, which is better suited for the Highlands than any other manufacture. But though such a plan were already established, it would be too slow in its operations to produce that immediate relief to the poor people that their present situation requires; for I have certain information that there are now persons traversing the islands to entice the poor people to go to America. I have, therefore, wrote to several persons, to endeavour to send information to all the places where the people are proposing to leave their native country to advertise them that they may have employment in the Lowlands, particularly in Glasgow, Paisley, and the towns and villages round them; and I have pledged myself to build houses at Lanark for 200 families, and to give them employment.

Several gentlemen in this place are forming a society to prevent emigrations, and your subscription will be thankfully received. I am confident that not a single person in Scotland, who is able and willing to work, has any occasion to leave their native country for want of the means of a comfortable subsistence; and the design of the society now forming here, is to direct the people in the Highlands who are under the necessity of leaving their own country, where to find employment without going to America. Could the people find employment in the Highlands it would be much better for them to remain there; but, as this is not the case, the best thing that can be done for them and for this country, is to invite all that cannot find employment to come here, and they will be provided for.[38b]

A sum of £3000 was raised to erect the mill and Dale's share was reported in the *Old Statistical Account* as a mere £200.[39] However, the evidence in Calder's thesis shows conclusively that[40] both Dale and MacIntosh each had shares of £300. By 1794 there were already ten houses round the mill. There were two weaving houses (one with a warehouse and 12 looms and another with 10 looms), a store, a washing house and a smithy. The mill was producing a type of cotton handkerchief but was in financial difficulties from the start. The expenditure on the mills amounted to £3053-1s-8½d, yet the capital only totalled £2300, and by 1795 the company had to borrow another £2500 to stay in business.

The parish had no poor's fund; farming was tremendously difficult; young men went south for work in the spring and summer and "were a burden on their friends the whole winter"; [41] no bridges were available to cross the river, and most of the minister's stipend was paid in meal and beer. Nevertheless, a cotton mill and two villages were erected. The *Old Statistical Account* notes that:

> "Instructed persons are sent from Glasgow to con-
> duct the work and to teach the natives of the country
> the arts of spinning and weaving." [42]

The minister at the time of writing expressed his doubts about the possible success of such a venture, arguing that to expect such people to live in "factory communities" and change their ways overnight was not likely to assure profit, although he recognised that "public spirit" was "the motive by which most of the partners have been induced to embark their property." [43]

The minister's fears proved to be well-founded. All the partners eventually withdrew, except MacIntosh and Dale, who tried to keep it going by applying for government aid. [44] Eventually Dale asked MacIntosh to sell the mill in 1804, and in 1806 it burned down and was never rebuilt. The destruction of the mill resulted in the gradual decay of the village. [45]

At roughly the same time as the founding of Spinningdale, Dale established a small mill in Oban:

> "Of late a small branch of the cotton manufacture
> was introduced into this quarter by Mr David Dale of
> Glasgow, but its progress has been greatly retarded by
> the dearth of fuel. That cause now being removed,
> other gentlemen of enterprise and public spirit have
> it in contemplation to establish works of the same
> kind." [46]

Exactly when this was established is unclear, as is the date of Dale's withdrawal from it. Finally, there is only one reference to a mill erected on the River Cree upstream from Newton Douglas. This was erected in 1783 at a cost of £10,000 by the firm of Douglas, Dale & McCall. [47]

The last cotton spinning venture in which Dale invested money was at Stanley, seven miles north of Perth on a bend of the River Tay. Once again, the exact date of his involvement is uncertain, but it was at "a later period in his life", according to the *Dictionary of Eminent Scotsmen*, and the same source states that it was Owen who advised him to become involved in the venture which Andrew Liddell [48] claimed was to lose Dale some £60,000.

In fact, Dale did not become involved financially with Stanley until 1803, [49] and in order to explain the loss of his money it is necessary to give a very brief history of the mill. George Dempster, the local M.P., had persuaded Arkwright, (who had been given the Freedom of the City of Perth), and others to put up money for the mill in 1785 on 70 acres of land feued from the Duke of Atholl. As in Spinningdale, men from Stanley went to Cromford to learn how to operate the machinery. In the event, Arkwright withdrew from the venture in 1787, but by 1795 the mill was employing 350 people, 300 of whom were women or children under 16, and there were 100 families in the village. The mills (one cotton and one flax) were valued at £10,500 — second only to those at New Lanark. However, the war and the rising price of cotton affected Stanley very badly, and when the flax mill was burned to the ground in 1799, the company was forced to put the mills on the market, which had an effect on the village.

One final attempt was made to resurrect the mills in 1802 when two Glasgow merchants, James Craig and James Mair, bought the business for £4600. By 1803 Mair had left and Dale had joined Craig, paying £1533 for the privilege. Since Dale left many of his business affairs at this time to Owen, it is reasonable to assume that he entered this partnership on Owen's advice. This advice proved extremely costly because these mills *never* made a profit and between 1803 and 1806, Dale supplied £24,270 of working capital in an attempt to keep the business going. In fact, after his death, the Dale Trustees advanced a further £15,996 until Owen finally withdrew from the venture in 1811 and the mills closed in 1814. [49] All in all, Stanley could be said to have cost Dale over £40,000. Thus, although Liddell's figure of £60,000 is inflated, this enterprise certainly cost Dale a fortune.

There is some scanty evidence that Dale was involved in two further business ventures, but details of these have proved very difficult to trace. On 1st May 1782, the following advertisement appeared in *The Glasgow Mercury*:

" 'To Shipmasters'
Vessels are wanted, during the Spring and Summer, to carry Easdale slates from the quarries to the Frith (sic) of Forth. Enquire at Messrs David Dale & Co. merchants, Glasgow, John Campbell, Esq., writer to the Signet, Edinburgh and Mr Archibald Campbell, Easdale, by Inverary."

A similar advertisement appeared the following week with two additions as follows: "the Friths of Forth and Clyde" and "N.B. As there is a demand for the slates, it is expected of those who are willing to freight their vessels that they will apply immediately."

I cannot say whether this was a long or short term commercial venture as so little is known about it.

It is much the same with the Barrowfield Coal Company. Dale was a partner in this company with Robert Tennant and David Todd, both of whom are listed as merchants in Glasgow. Todd was, I think, a partner in Todd, Shortridge & Co., linen printers in Argyle Street and was also a partner in Todd & Stevenson, cotton spinners, who had mills at Bridge of Weir and Springfield near Glasgow. Tennant or Tennent was probably the partner in John and Robert Tennent, the brewers and maltmen in Glasgow.

Dale is supposed to have lost some £20,000 in this venture, owing to the fact that the company never reached any large amounts of coal because the soil was a running quicksand. This is extremely difficult to verify as there appear to be no extant records of the company. During Dale's lifetime, mining was certainly taking place on the Barrowfield estate with the proviso that no pit was to be sunk within 100 yards of James Dunlop's cotton mill (which was then sited on the estate) but whether Dale was involved in this is not clear. It seems likely that he was, given that both Liddell and the *Dictionary of Eminent Scotsmen* mention it, and it appears from a contemporary plan that the Dale family, if not Dale himself, owned property in the area. [50] Similarly, a map dated 1823 [51] shows a working 4000 feet long from Barrowfield, west under Glasgow Green almost to the river. It runs near the east end of Monteith Row and is only 700 yards from Dale's house in Charlotte Street. This seam is named "Dale's Dyke", although it is not clear whether this is because of Dale's active involvement with the Barrowfield Coal Company or merely because he was still a well-remembered figure in the area.

He was also involved in "prospecting" or quarrying for coal and sandstone in Carluke and Lanark, but apparently this was unsuccessful too. He was also permitted to take heather and divots for thatching. [51b]

The latter part of Dale's business career, apart from his investment in the Stanley Mills, saw the sale of the cotton mills which had made him so famous. This began in 1799 with the sale of New Lanark to Owen and his partners for £66,000 payable over 20 years at 5% interest. [52] Owen, of course, was to be his son-in-law, and at that time Owen had capital of £3000, a sum which Dale matched in his dowry for Caroline. Thus Owen doubled his capital, gained access to plenty of trading capital through Dale's association with the Royal Bank, and purchased the famous New Lanark mills.

Dale's active association with the bank ceased in the following year and John More from an Edinburgh branch was appointed in Dale's place. More himself is an interesting character. He became, after 1800, a major partner in the Stanley Mills and is reported [53] as living extravagantly, apparently trying to emulate Dale's success using the Royal Bank's money and running up a debt of £94,267 in the process.[54]   Dale certainly knew him and More became the factor for the Dale Trustees after Dale's death.

Catrine mills were sold to James Finlay in 1801, followed by Spinningdale in 1804.   According to Owen,[55]   Dale never visited Spinningdale and instructed his son-in-law to inspect it on his behalf. Owen found the place "unfavourable for extension or for a permanent establishment" [56] and advised selling it off along with the Stanley Mills. Thus (again according to Owen):

> "These sales released Mr Dale from much anxiety and allowed him to pass the remainder of his life more quietly and much more to his satisfaction." [57]

References and Notes

1   Senex (R. Reid), *Glasgow Past and Present*, Glasgow 1884, Vol. 3, p. 372.
1b   W.G. Black, *David Dale's House*, Glasgow, Maclehose, 1908, p. 12.
2   A. Liddell, *Memoir of David Dale Esq.*, Glasgow 1854, p. 164.
2b   S.G. Checkland, *Scottish Banking: A History 1695-1973*, Collins, 1975, p. 145.
3   *The Three Banks Review* No. 45, March 1960, p. 42.
4   N. Munro, *The History of the Royal Bank of Scotland 1727-1927*, Edinburgh, Clark, 1928, p. 155.
5   *The Three Banks Review*, op. cit.
6   N. Munro, op. cit.
7   *The Three Banks Review*, op. cit.
8   Ibid. p. 34.

9   G. Parker, *The Emergence of Modern Finance in Europe 1500-*
       1730, in *The Fontana Economic History of Europe*, Vol 2, edited
       C.M. Cipolla, Collins, 1974, p. 540.
10   Senex (R. Reid), *Old Glasgow and Its Environs*, Glasgow 1864, p.
       353, refers to Sterling & Sons credit.
11   *The Three Banks Review*, op. cit.
12   N. Munro, op. cit., pp. 150-1.
13   These letters are held by the Royal Bank of Scotland, but are
       referred to extensively in S.G. Checkland, op. cit.
14   S.G. Checkland, op. cit., p. 230.
15   A. Brown, *The History of Glasgow*, Glasgow 1797, Bk. 3, p. 225,
       refers to Dempster's origin in the county of Sutherland where he
       was also a landowner.
16   J. Butt, *The Industrial Archeology of Scotland*, David & Charles,
       1967, pp. 64-7.
       J.R. Hume, *The Industrial Archaeology of Scotland*, Batsford Ltd.,
       1976, Vol. 1.
       See also D. Bremner, *Industries of Scotland*, Edinburgh, 1869, p.
       279: "The Rothesay mill was not long in being acquired by Mr
       Dale." However, I can find no other reference to Dale's involve-
       ment in the Rothesay mill.
17   E. Baines, *History of Cotton Manufacture in Great Britain*, Lon-
       don, 1835, pp. 120-198 for a full description of the process.
18   Cited in R.S. Fitton & A.P. Wadsworth, *The Strutts and the*
       Arkwrights 1758-1830, Manchester University Press, 1958, p. 84.
19   Ibid., p. 87.
20   G. Stewart, *Curiosities of Glasgow Citizenship*, Glasgow, 1881,
       pp. 50-52.
21   Ibid.
22   J. Sinclair (Ed.), *Old Statistical Account for Scotland*, Vol. XV.
23   J.R. Hume, *The Industrial Archaeology of New Lanark*, p. 218,
       in J. Butt (Ed.), *Robert Owen Prince of Cotton Spinners*, David &
       Charles, 1971.
24   R. Alison, *The Anecdotage of Glasgow*, Glasgow 1892, pp.
       185-9.
25   N. Munro, op. cit., p. 152: "This time Dale was the partner with
       the money. Arkwright contributed to the enterprise the waterframe
       spinning machine."

26   Letter from Dale to Alexander dated 7th April 1788: "I have received a letter from Sir Richard Arkwright advising me that he has sent off two boxes containing plates, wheels and rollers for two spinning frames, 48 spindles directed for me at Mauchline by Dumfries." Mitchell Library, MS 63.

27   New Lanark Visitors Book 1795-99, Glasgow University Archives.

28   R. Owen, *The Life of Robert Owen by Himself*, London, Knight & Co., 1971, p. 46.

29   *Old Statistical Account*, Vol. XII, p. 114.

30   Footnote in *Dictionary of Eminent Scotsmen*. The linen tape was exported to America and became known as Scotch Tape.

31   A. Cullen, *Adventures in Socialism*, Glasgow, J. Smith, 1910, p. 10.

32   Dale to Alexander 1781, Mitchell Library, MS. 63.

33   *James Finlay & Co., Manufacturers & East India Merchants 1750-1950*, Glasgow 1954, p. 55.

34   *Old Statistical Account*, Vol. XX, p. 177.

35   Ibid.

36   Ibid.

37   Dale to Alexander, 23rd January 1792. Dale says he is sorry to learn that four thatched-roof cottages burned down and recommends slate roofs if the buildings are worth the expense. "I shall write for a fire engine if you please, but there is not the least chance of our getting one from the insurers." He complains that the engine and six dozen buckets at New Lanark cost him "above £150". And Dale to Alexander, 6th June 1793. Both in Mitchell Library, MS. 63.

38   S. Mechie, *The Church and Scottish Social Development 1780-1870*, O.U.P., 1960, pp. 10-11.

38b   Transcript of a letter from David Dale of Glasgow to Colonel Dalrymple of Fordell, on the subject of Emigrations, published in the *Scots Magazine*, 1791. I am grateful to Lorna Davidson Education Officer at New Lanark, for providing me with a copy of this letter.

39   *Old Statistical Account*, Vol IV, Creich, p. 352.

40   S.B. Calder, *Industrial Archaeology of Scotland: A Scottish Highland Economy 1700-1900*, M.Litt. Thesis, Strathclyde 1974, pp. 165-178. Much of my information on Spinningdale comes from this thesis.

41   *Old Statistical Account*, op. cit., p. 343.

42   Ibid., p. 346.

43   Ibid., p. 351.

44   G. Stewart, *Curiosities*, op. cit., pp. 81-2.

45   *New Statistical Account for Scotland*, Edinburgh, Blackwood & Sons, Vol. XV, p. 20.

46   *Old Statistical Account*, Vol. II, p. 132.

47   *History of Lanark and a Guide to the Scenery*, 3rd edition, 1835.

48   A Liddell, *Memoir of David Dale Esq.*, Glasgow 1854, p. 167.

49   A.J. Cooke, *The Early Development of Stanley* in *Stanley, Its History and Development*, University of Dundee Extra Mural Dept., Dundee, 1977, pp. 11-18.

50   Plan of the road leading from St Mungo's Street to Barrowfield Bridge showing the Royal Boundary, by W. Pollok, 1811.

51   McLellend's Map of Barrowfield and Coal Workings, 1823.

51b   History of Lanark etc., op. cit.

52   J. Butt, " Robert Owen as Businessman"in J. Butt (Ed.) *Robert Owen Prince of Cotton Spinners*, David & Charles, 1971.

53   Senex (R. Reid), *Glasgow Past & Present*, Glasgow 1884, Vol. II, p. 129: "On Saturdays and holidays a splendid equipage with a black servant . . . drove up to the bank to convey the manager to his rural home at Wellshot, which he had erected and surrounded with a vinery, a flower garden, and romantic walks and bowling green at an expense of £17,000.''

54   S.G. Checkland, op. cit, p. 298.

55   Owen's *Life*, p. 72-3.

56   Ibid. p. 75.

57   Ibid. p. 78.

"A GENIAL, HUMOROUS MAN"

I have called Dale a businessman, but to appreciate his importance fully, it is necessary to set him in the context of the Glasgow of his day and to fill in some general background.

Glasgow in the year 1785, for example, is described [1] as having open ground everywhere with extensive gardens behind the houses in Saltmarket, Gallowgate and the Trongate. It was possible to take pleasant country walks to Camlachie, Cowcaddens, Cranstonhill and Crossmyloof. The working classes, including Dale's employees, worked very long hours every day with no full holidays except New Year's Day and Fair Saturday. There was little entertainment for them except an occasional fair or public hanging. The upper classes had, theoretically, more time to enjoy themselves but J.O. Mitchell writes that they were "little better off":

"There were a few dinners at three, or in the highest circles, at four o'clock . . ." [1]

but these did not yet consist of more than one course.

Travelling meant the use of horses, and this turned long journeys into major expeditions. The mail, for example, left the Saracen's Head Inn in Glasgow at 9 a.m. and went to Edinburgh, Moffat, Carlisle, then a change of coach to Ripon, Leeds and finally London. All this could take up to ten days. Glasgow to Edinburgh took the best part of a day and cost seven shillings, which was very expensive. Coaches left Glasgow at 2 a.m. every day for Greenock and at 12 noon five days a week for Ireland.

Two years later in 1787, there was the famous weavers' strike in Calton over the manufacturers' refusal to grant an advance on wages. On 3rd September, a mob was burning cloth in the Drygate when the magistrates arrived with men from the 39th Infantry Regiment. The Riot Act was read but this had no effect on the crowd and the soldiers opened fire, killing three people. Not surprisingly, this caused huge anger and bitterness and the funeral was attended by 6000 people.

Hangings were carried out at Castle Yard until 1787 when the site was moved to the Tolbooth Steeple. Hangings were not nearly as common as popular legend would have us believe. Between 1784–7 a total of 12 people were hanged, usually for the crimes of murder, robbery, housebreaking or forgery.

Against this rather gloomy picture of Glasgow, however, has to be set the Glasgow of trade, commerce and progress. The city's population grew from 45,000 in 1783 to 83,769 in 1801, the year of the official Census. This was of course a reflection of Glasgow's growing importance as a commercial centre. The Chamber of Commerce, with the foundation of which Dale was closely associated, [2] had been established as early as 1783 and was one of the first in Britain. It was set up primarily as a reaction to the commercial distress caused by the war with America and found itself involved with import and export duties, the quality of home-produced goods and the distribution of money for manufacturers who had hit hard times.

In the same year, the Royal Bank began trading in Glasgow (again an indication of the city's importance as a commercial centre) and a Directory appeared, listing the names of the city's merchants, ministers, academics and shopkeepers. The Forth and Clyde Canal was completed in 1790 and the River Clyde itself was deepened to accommodate larger vessels. At Port Glasgow and Greenock, ships left for such far-flung places as New York, Boston, St Lucia, Antigua, Jamaica and Denmark, loaded with herrings, brick, slate, limestone, timber, meal and cotton-spinning machinery. They brought back to the city such delights as tobacco, sugar, coffee and rum, and of course as a result of all this trade, the shipbuilding industry grew.

In the city itself, new industries were starting up: brewing in Wellpark, tanning in the Gallowgate, chemical manufacture in what is now Springburn, shoemaking in the Saltmarket.

The gentleman of the day could have his coffee in his own "club" in the Tontine Rooms, where he had the choice of several newspapers — *The Journal, The Courier, The Mercury* or *The Glasgow Advertiser* which changed its name in 1802 to *The Glasgow Herald*. If he was lucky, the gentleman's coffee might have been made with water from one of the new water carts, rather than from the private (or public) wells.

By the late 1790's, his conversations over coffee might have included the new proposal to levy a tax to pay for a regular police force with a Chief of Police to be appointed at £200 per annum; a clerk at £85; a treasurer at £80; three sergeants at £40 each; nine officers at £30 each; and 68 watchmen at 10/- per week. [3] This new tax would also have to pay for new street lamps and new sentry boxes for the watchmen. His conversation over, the gentleman might decide to return home to one of the new "suburbs" of Gorbals or Tradeston in the south of the city, Finnieston or Anderston in the west or Cowcaddens in the north.

It is against this background of increasing trade and prosperity in Glasgow that Dale must be seen. His business successes mirrored Glasgow's, but he was much more than a hard-headed businessman. He was also concerned with the welfare of his fellow man, and for contemporary observers, this seems to have been one of the most striking aspects of his character.

In the 1780's and 90's Dale's career was at its height. He was a well-known public figure and many stories (some true, some apocryphal) grew up around him. Most comments had to do with either his physical appearance or his benevolent nature.

Of his appearance:

"In person he was short and corpulent and the complete beau ideal of a Glasgow Bailie in living and genuine reality." [4]

"He was a model old Glasgow worthy." [5]

1.   2.   3.   4.   5.
THE MORNING WALK.

Glasgow, Published as the Act directs April 1795.

Kay's Morning Walk
1. David Dale.   2. John Wallace.   3. Robert Dreghorn.
4. Unknown.   5. Laurence Coulter.

Many examples are cited of his work as a benevolent magistrate:

"He won the golden opinions of his fellow citizens
as he tempered justice with mercy."[6]

Of his genial nature:

> "Withal, he was a genial, humorous man. He was
> given to hospitality and he would sing an old Scotch
> song with such feeling as to bring tears to the eyes." [7]

Finally:

> "He was, in short, respected by the wealthy and be-
> loved by the poor," [8]

and on his deathbed asked his fellow Old Scotch Independents

> "for forgiveness if on any occasion he had given them
> offence and prayed for a blessing on them." [9]

All this praise for Dale, however justified, does rather
present him as an amiable and slightly eccentric old gentleman.
This view should be avoided. He most certainly was benevolent
and had a social conscience, but he was nobody's fool, particularly in the business world, and on occasions he could be quite
ruthless. The account of his business career has shown that he
got rid of Paterson and Arkwright when their usefulness to him
was over, and when Monteith "begged and intreated him in the
most earnest manner to annul the sale of the Blantyre Mill" [10]
because of the recession in the cotton trade, Dale refused point
blank and Monteith only just managed to survive that year.

A symbol of Dale's success and prosperity was his famous
mansion in Charlotte Street, which unfortunately no longer exists.
The ground on which it was built was bought in the first instance
by Archibald Paterson in response to an advertisement in *The
Glasgow Mercury* on 17th February 1780:

> "Ground for building to be sold. That, upon Wednes-
> day 1st of March 1780, there is to be sold, by public
> roup, within the house of Mr Buchanan, vintner,

Saracen's Head, Glasgow, that piece of ground in
Merkdailly, in the Gallowgate of Glasgow. The progress of writs and conditions of sale will be seen in
the hand of Thomas Buchanan of Boquhan, writer in
Glasgow."

Paterson bought these Merkdailly lands and opened a street
which ran through their full length, from the Gallowgate to the
Low Green in the east end of the city (see map on following
page). This he called Charlotte Street in honour of her then
Majesty, Queen Charlotte, wife of George III. Sasine (legal
possession) followed on 17th March 1780 and Paterson sold part
of it to Dale on 23rd June of the same year:

"I have resolved to lay off and accordingly have laid
off and appropriated the greatest part of the foresaid
grounds for the purposes of a regular street to be
named Charlotte Street . . . And seeing that David
Dale, Merchant in Glasgow hath now made payment
to me of the sum of £233.16s. Sterling . . . I do here-
by sell, dispone and make over from me and in favour
of the said David Dale . . ."[11]

Work could now begin on Dale's house and it took some
two and a half years and £6000 to complete the task. Robert
Adam, appointed architect and designer, was known especially
for the elegance of his interior design.

The plan of the house[12] shows that there were two storeys
at the front and four at the back, which included a kitchen and
basement and an attic at the top of the house. On the two main
floors were four large rooms (each about 24ft. x 16ft.) facing the
street and these served principally as a dining-room, library and
two drawing-rooms. The octagonal room on the second floor was
Dale's own personal study.

On each side of the main building were one storey "wings"
with their own entrances and these were probably used as ser-

Taken from a Facsimile of a Map which appeared in *The Glasgow Magazine of 1783*

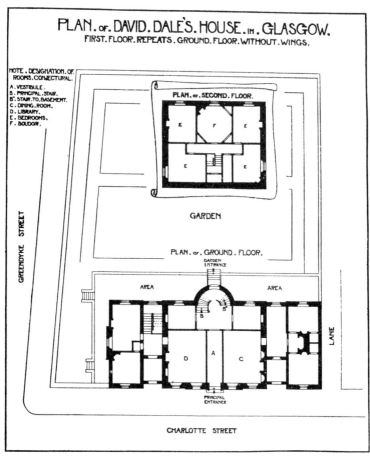

PLAN. of. DAVID. DALE'S. HOUSE. in. GLASGOW.

FIRST. FLOOR. REPEATS. GROUND. FLOOR. WITHOUT. WINGS.

NOTE. DESIGNATION. OF.
ROOMS. CONJECTURAL.

A. VESTIBULE.
B. PRINCIPAL. STAIR.
B". STAIR. TO. BASEMENT.
C. DINING. ROOM.
D. LIBRARY.
E. BEDROOMS.
F. BOUDOIR.

PLAN. of. SECOND. FLOOR.

GREENDYKE STREET

GARDEN

PLAN. of. GROUND. FLOOR.

GARDEN ENTRANCE

AREA   AREA

LANE

PRINCIPAL ENTRANCE

CHARLOTTE STREET

vants' quarters or for conducting informal business transactions. The gardens illustrated were in fact a good deal larger because Dale bought another piece of land behind the house in 1784 and further extended his land in the same year when he bought 1254 square yards of the Eaglesham Croft land, also at the back of the house.

There was a fireplace in each room, including the wine cellar, because there was no such thing as damp-coursing in those days. Even so, the house would still be damp, and it was a fairly common occurrence for the cellar and kitchen to be flooded out when the Camlachie Burn overflowed. On one such occasion, there was a great panic because Dale had invited some fellow Directors of the Royal Bank for dinner. Nothing daunted, he sent out servants to ask whether his neighbours would object to his staff using their kitchens to prepare the food, and the situation was saved. That is, except for the wine. Rather than stretch his neighbours' kindness too far (and in doing so deprive his guests of the fruits of his famous wine cellar) "a seafaring man" [13] was brought in to wade through the cellar and Dale's eldest daughter, Carolina, had to climb on top of this gentleman's shoulders to reach some of the bottles.

Adam Fireplace in David Dale's House

Dinners, it should be said, were given frequently at Charlotte Street, as one might expect of such a famous and wealthy merchant. They normally took place in mid-afternoon and it was the custom until the late 1780's to have all the food placed on the table at one time, rather than have separate "courses" served. At that time, the dinners would end before sunset, but this custom gradually changed with the introduction of street lights and a proper police force.

However, Charlotte Street was also Dale's home, though information about his wife and children is scanty and it is not possible to build up much of a picture of his family life. The family tree on page 112 shows the members of his family, but it will be noted that the dates of their births and deaths are not available, with the exception of Anne Caroline. Dale is reported in most sources as having had five children, but in fact he had seven, two of whom died in infancy (a daughter in 1783 and a son in 1789).

The house in Charlotte Street, where, as far as I can ascertain, all his children (except Caroline) were born, also saw the wedding of Anne Caroline (Carolina) to Robert Owen on 30th September 1799. Rather than conduct the wedding himself (which he could have done as a pastor in the Old Scotch Independents) Dale asked a Church of Scotland minister, the Reverend Mr Balfour, to perform the ceremony. Apparently, Balfour merely asked Owen and Carolina if they took each other in marriage and, after they nodded, pronounced them man and wife. Owen reports [14] that he was surprised at how brief the ceremony was and the minister replied that it was normally longer because he usually explained to the couple their duties in marriage and often gave "a long exhortation".

> "But," said Balfour, "I would not presume to do this
> with Mr Dale's children while he lived and was present,
> knowing that he must have previously satisfied him-
> self in giving them such advice as seemed necessary
> and sufficient."

A map published in 1807 [15] shows Charlotte Street in greater detail and also includes the names of Dale's neighbours, assuming that they were already living there in 1806, the year of his death. All these names appear in lists of Merchants and Guild

A Section of Fleming's Map of Glasgow published in 1807

Brethren, but of course there are several individuals named "James Craig", "James Black" and so on, and it is difficult to say whether these residents of Charlotte Street are the merchants referred to. In any case, they must all have been fairly wealthy men to have lived in Charlotte Street. Some twenty years before the publication of this map, Dale's neighbours were easier to identify: David Black (possibly the same person as the David Black of 1807) was a tobacco merchant; James Jackson was the Postmaster; William Taylor was minister of the High Church; Archibald Coats, Thomas Bell and Walter Ewing were "merchants"; James Jeffrey was an architect and cabinet maker, and James Scott was a wholesale dealer in Irish linens. Finally, there was Archibald Paterson, Dale's sometime partner.[16] It is clear, then, that Charlotte Street was the dwelling-place of wealthy middle-class citizens, and Dale's house appears to have been one of the largest in the street. Not shown on the map of 1807 is the big iron gate at the south end which was used to keep the street private. This certainly existed in the 1780's, but may have been removed as the city expanded and the number of streets grew.

As well as Charlotte Street, Dale had a country house, Rosebank, near Cambuslang. He bought this in 1800 and spent a great deal of time there during the last six years of his life. It was at Rosebank that he died on 17th March 1806.

After his death, Charlotte Street was retained by the family and it seems that Jean Maxwell Dale and Margaret Dale divided their time between Charlotte Street, Rosebank and Braxfield House, where Owen and Carolina lived. Dale's other daughters, Mary and Julia, had both married ministers and left the neighbourhood. The house in Charlotte Street was finally sold in 1827 to a Mr Moses McCulloch, merchant in Glasgow, for £2200. When McCulloch died, his widow sold it to a Director of the Eye Infirmary in 1852, and the house actually became the Eye Infirmary, Dale's octagonal study being used as the operating theatre. The Infirmary was transferred to Berkeley Street in 1874 but Dale's house was retained as a Dispensary. It subsequently belonged to the Education Authority, who had the building demolished in the 1950's to make room for an extension to an adjacent school. [17] The extension was never built.

David Dale's House as the Eye Infirmary
Photograph taken in 1900

References and Notes

1 J.O. Mitchell, *Old Glasgow Essays*, Glasgow, Maclehose, 1905, pp. 323-4.

2 Dale was one of the founder members in 1783.

3 McGregor, *History of Glasgow*, Glasgow, 1881, pp. 381-2.

4 Alison, *The Anecdotage of Glasgow*, Glasgow, 1892, p. 186.

5 Ibid., p. 185.

6 Ibid., p. 185.

7 W.G. Black, *David Dale's House* in *Transactions of the Regality Club*, Fourth Series, Glasgow, 1912, p. 95.

8 *Book of Glasgow Anecdotage*, Glasgow 1912.

9 Stewart's *Curiosities of Glasgow Citizenship*, pp. 134-5.

10 Senex (R. Reid), *Glasgow Past and Present*, Vol. II, p. 51.

11 W.G. Black, op. cit., pp. 104-5.

12 Ibid., p. 112.

13 Ibid., p. 113.

14 Robert Owen, *Life*, p. 55.

15 Fleming's map of Glasgow, 1807.

16 Jones' *Directory*, Glasgow, Graham, 1868.

17 Frank Worsdall, *The City That Disappeared*, Richard Drew, Glasgow, 1981, p. 28.

EDUCATION AND SOCIAL PROVISION

When Dale sold New Lanark to Robert Owen in 1799, he sold not only a profitable enterprise, but a place which had had from its outset a tradition of providing good accommodation and living conditions and also a school. What Owen provided was undoubtedly superior as far as schooling was concerned, but the credit has to go to Dale for establishing a school which served the community surrounding the mills.

It must also be borne in mind, however, that the 'factory community' idea was not Dale's invention. Arkwright had built houses, machine shops, inns, a chapel, roads and bridges as well as a mill at Cromford, all of this some 15 years before the water wheels turned at New Lanark. At that time some children at Cromford worked from 6 a.m. till 7 p.m. with only one hour for dinner and no time allowed for breakfast, until the demand for cotton appeared to fall and daylight working was resumed. This was stated by Archibald Buchanan,[1] and Arkwright's son confirms it, giving the children's ages as seven or eight.[2] In Cromford, Arkwright also provided a ball and a feast at his house for the work people twice a year and gave bonuses to some of the principal workmen. He provided a village market and by 1785 had got round to providing a Sunday school for the children.[3]

His original partner at Cromford, Jedediah Strutt, had also attempted to establish a 'community' round his mills at Belper. He had built some houses near the original North Mill during 1784—86 and "Long Row", a similar creation to Dale's Long Row at New Lanark, was built along with the West Mill which began spinning in 1796.

Four months before Arkwright built his Sunday School at Cromford, Strutt had built one at Belper:

"We hear from Belpar (sic) that Mr Strutt has, (with

a liberality which does honour to the human heart)
entirely at his own expense, instituted a Sunday
School for the benefit of all the youth of both sexes
employed in his cotton mill at that town; and
provides them with all necessary books etc., for
learning to read and write . . . An example worthy of
imitation . . . it becomes the duty of every thinking
person . . . to hold forth an assisting hand . . . to stop
the tide of Immorality." [4]

It should be noted that these Sunday Schools at Belper and
Cromford have to be seen in the context of the huge expansion in
the number of Sunday Schools in the late eighteenth century.
The Sunday School in Manchester opened in 1784 and trebled its
numbers to some 5500 by 1788, and the total number of children
attending Sunday Schools in 1787 was approximately 250,000.
The Scottish picture was somewhat different, owing to the
tradition of the parish school and its emphasis on 'reading' in
order to be able to read the Bible. Sunday Schools as such were
only really organised after 1800 by evangelists like David Stow.
    All of this has to be borne in mind before it can be claimed
that Dale's treatment of his workers was entirely original. Certainly, the provision of day schooling was relatively new, but the
principle of the 'factory community' was not.
    Even the provision of day schooling itself may not have
been revolutionary, since it is just possible that William Gillespie's
cotton mill in North Woodside (1784) had a school attached to it
from the beginning. I have been unable to find out when this
school was built. It is quite possible, however, that it was in
operation before the New Lanark one. It was described in *The
Old Statistical Account* as a "charity school":

" . . . There is a charity school in the Calton supported
by Mr David Dale; and one in the mill at Woodside,
supported by Mr Gillespie, for the instruction of the
children attending his cotton mill." [5]

Evidence of a community as well as a school is also provided by the *Old Statistical Account:*

"This [i.e. the cotton mill] with the people engaged in the bleachfield and otherwise, has made Woodside a considerable village, while it has become a seat of plenty and comfort, the happy consequence of industry and manufacture. Sensible to the advantages of religion and good morals, to promote the industry and happiness of the people, the benevolent proprietor pays particular attention to these. He has not only engaged a master to teach children through the week, to read, but he has also fitted up, and supports at his own expense, a place for public worship on the Lord's Day." [6]

Thus it can be seen that Dale's efforts at New Lanark were indeed improvements, but improvements on a model which had its beginnings in Cromford in England and possibly Woodside in Glasgow.

Similarly, the general notion of "charity schooling" was also well established by this time. The clearest definition of a "charity school" is to be found in an article by Joan Simon which looks not at Glasgow but at Leicestershire.[7] Her argument, however, is just as valid for Glasgow. She argues that there was not a "charity school movement", but that there were many different kinds of school with various degrees of "charity" associated with them. The only real charity schools were those which were non fee-paying and which had as their aim the rescuing "from idleness and irreligion the unemployed poor from 7—12", i.e. not a parish school with free places. The school also had to set them on the path to a useful working life, normally by helping the children to find employment. The schools also had to provide clothes, food and books.

Now when this model of 18th Century charity schooling is applied to Glasgow, very few genuine "charity" schools stand out.

Hutcheson's Hospital, founded 1641, certainly maintained, clothed and educated boys over 9 years of age and bound them as apprentices, but only if these boys were sons of Burgesses and if they had attended an English school (i.e. a school which taught reading and some grammar) for six months before entering Hutcheson's. The idea of a free education for those who could afford to pay for it does not really equate with the notion of "charity".

The only institution which came close to Simon's charity school was the Town's Hospital, which clothed, fed, educated, nursed, lodged and employed pauper children. Even here, however, this must be set against the fact that it also housed lunatics, geriatrics and sick adults.

Of Dale's "charity school" (or rather the school to which Dale subscribed) in the Calton, nothing is known. New Lanark, on the other hand, is slightly more accessible. Here the children were fed, clothed, lodged, employed and educated and there was less of the workhouse about it than at the Town's Hospital. No fees were charged for the apprentices and it would seem that New Lanark comes very close to a Simon-type charity school. Nevertheless, fees *were* charged for the rest of the children, and it could be argued that by not paying the apprentice (pauper) children any wages, Dale was in effect charging them for their board and education.

The point is that the idea of a factory community was not new; perhaps even day schooling in mills was not new; neither was the idea of "charity schooling". What *was* new was Dale's expansion of these ideas to produce a thriving community with a thriving school as well as providing charity for his pauper children. As I shall show, he provided a great deal for the people of New Lanark — much more than any other mill owner. Here at New Lanark, 'community', 'school' and 'charity' came together for the first time.

Number Four Mill was used "as a store room for cotton wool, as workshops for the different tradesmen employed; and as a boarding house for 275 children who have no parents here, and who get their maintenance, education and clothing for work." [8]

These were pauper children brought from the Town's Hospital in Glasgow, of which Dale became a Director in 1787, (see Chapter 5), and the Charity Workhouse in Edinburgh. They were called "apprentices" to distinguish them from the children who stayed with their parents in the village. From the statistics [9] it can be deduced that of 1157 people actually employed in the manufacturing process, there were 795 children (68% of the workforce), of whom 275 were boarded in Number Four Mill, 103 lived in the Burgh of Lanark, leaving over 400 living with parents in the village at New Lanark.

One explanation of why Dale, in common with many English mill owners (with the possible exception of Arkwright) [10] used pauper children is offered by 'Alfred' (Samuel Kydd) in 1857. Although not always a reliable source, Kydd does shed some light on why the Lanark people were so opposed at first to Dale's attempts to buy the land from Lord Justice McQueen of Braxfield:

> "For a long period it was by the working people themselves considered to be disgraceful to any father who allowed his child to enter the factory . . . It was not until the conditions of portions of the working classes had been reduced that it became the custom with working men to eke out the means of their subsistence by sending their children to the mills. Until that sad and calamitous custom prevailed the factories in England were worked by 'stranger children' gathered together from the workhouses." [11]

Mill owners made a 'deal' with the local overseer for the acquisition of children to work in the mills. The overseer was, according to the original Constitution, the "one person with the principal superintendence" of the workhouse. [12] . All the staff and inmates were responsible to him and he was responsible for

ensuring that all the inmates were catered for according to the
rules, and he supervised the day to day running of the institution.
(The title was later changed to 'Preceptor' and then 'Manager'.)

"Alfred" goes on to mention some of the horrific circumstances in which these children often found themselves. Dale,
however, is quoted as an exception. His 'deal' with the overseer
was a simple one: "to undertake to feed, lodge and clothe
them." [13] The children were aged 5–8 and worked a 7–9 year
apprenticeship. A full breakdown of the ages of the children
is given in the *Old Statistical Account*, Vol. XV, p. 37:

Ages of the children employed in the New Lanark Mill in 1793

Age	No.
6	5
7	33
8	71
9	95
10	93
11	64
12	99
13	92
14	71
15	60
16	69
17	35

No mention of education is made in this 'deal' with the
overseer.

Dale certainly appears to have met his commitment in full.
The children housed in Number Four Mill were given regular
meals consisting of porridge and milk for breakfast, barley broth
for dinner,

"and as much beef is boiled as will allow 7 ounces
English apiece each day to one half of the children,
the other half get cheese and bread after their broth." [14]

Thus,

> "They dine alternately upon cheese and butchermeat,
> with barley bread or potatoes; and now and then in
> the proper season they have a dinner of herring and
> potatoes." [14]

Sometimes in winter the breakfast was "a composition of molasses and beer" instead of porridge. [15]

The apprentices mixed with the other children in the mill from 6 a.m. − 7 p.m., where they were employed in reeling or picking the cotton or mending any broken strands. The small fine hands of the women and children were well suited to this type of work. During their day at the mill, they had half an hour off for breakfast at 9 a.m. and one hour off for dinner at 2 p.m.[16] They worked until 7 p.m., "after which they attend the school at the expense of the proprietor till 9." [17]

Reports of the school are, in places, a little confusing. The *Old Statistical Account* quotes the number of teachers as ten: three "professed teachers" who taught during the day those children who were too young to work (possibly those under six years of age − see list on preceding page) and seven assistants "who attend in the evenings, one of whom teaches writing." [18] This was written in 1793 and accords with an article in the Annual Register of the previous year, in which it is stated that "ten schoolmasters are daily employed in their tuition." [19]

Thomas Garnett, Professor of Natural Philosophy and Chemistry at the Royal Institution, in his *Observations on a Tour through the Highlands* in 1800, quotes ten teachers, and although the flyleaf of the book is dated 1811, the article on New Lanark appears to have been written before 1796 (when Dale quotes sixteen teachers), or else Garnett's information is based on the *Old Statistical Account* of 1793. [20] Nevertheless, he does give some interesting information about New Lanark, supposedly based on what he saw there: [21]

> " . . . On going into the day school we heard some

little boys read in a very superior manner. In the
evening these three masters are assisted by seven
others, one of whom teaches writing. There is likewise a person who teaches sewing to the girls, and
another who teaches church music. The teachers have
written instructions, pointing out how far they are to
carry forward their scholars, before they are transferred to the next higher class. At dinner the masters
preside over the boys at table, performing the office
of chaplains and conduct them on Sundays to divine
worship, where they sometimes receive instruction
from their benevolent master. In the evening of Sunday, all the masters attend to teach, and give religious
and moral instruction."

The religious meetings were conducted in a meeting house
used by Dale's own sect, the Old Scotch Independents. It is
possible that this was a separate building, but it could have been
an area set aside for the purpose in Number Four Mill or New
Buildings.

The "curriculum" was more advanced than the one provided by either Arkwright or Strutt. Their schools were Sunday
Schools only (morning and afternoon) which focused on reading
and writing, interrupted by a compulsory visit to church, although
by 1801 it is reported [22] that children were attending "in the
weekdays as well". The New Lanark curriculum compares fav-
ourably with that offered in the so-called "charity schools" in
Glasgow. For example the sons (not daughters) of middle class
Burgesses at Hutcheson's were being taught the three R's, grammar
and church music, and were clothed twice a year.[23] New Lanark
did not have grammar, as far as I can ascertain, but both boys and
girls were educated, poor or not, the girls also being taught a
practical skill such as sewing, and they did not require to show
evidence of attendance at an 'English' school. The Town's Hospital had a similar curriculum.[24] (See Chapter 5.)   The children
were taught the three R's and church music as well as practical

skills like tambouring muslin (embroidering on a frame), hygiene and so on. Religion was taught in the form of catechising and it is not clear whether Dale used this method of religious instruction. New Lanark had much better social conditions than the Town's Hospital, and many more teachers.

The school at New Lanark was attended by children from the village as well. A clearer picture of what was happening in the "schools" is given by Dale himself in 1796 when the number of teachers had risen to sixteen and the number of pupils to 507.[25] At most, half an hour after supper saw the beginning of the classes. Thirteen teachers were employed to teach reading, two to teach writing and one to teach the pupils how to "figure". In addition, there was one teacher who taught sewing and one who occasionally taught church music. Thus the total number of teachers was *eighteen*, although the last two were probably part-time.

The mode of teaching required the division of the pupils into eight classes, with class number 8 being the 'highest' or top class. The number of scholars in each class is shown below:[26]

Class 1	65	Class 5	44
Class 2	85	Class 6	44
Class 3	76	Class 7	51
Class 4	65	Class 8	80

Each class was assigned "one or more teachers, as the numbers in that stage of advancement may require" and a kind of "scheme of work" was issued for each class,

> "which so soon as they have accomplished, the scholars are transferred to the next higher class, and the teacher receives a small premium for everyone so qualified."[26]

This suggests that the grading of the classes was based on the ability of the children. Within each class itself, pupils were encouraged to compete with each other:

"In their respective classes, the teachers promote
emulation in the usual way, by making the top of the
class the post of honour, which is still farther kept up
by the distribution of rewards every half year to such
as, from an account taken once a fortnight, appear to
have been most frequently uppermost." [26]

The Manager of the mill also had a duty to report back to
the Workhouse on the progress of the child employees. Strictly
speaking, this was unnecessary, since the children were "bound"
to New Lanark for a period of time. However, the Workhouse
Managers had to be satisfied with the terms and conditions if
they were to supply any more children. Such reports give an
interesting insight into the achievements and future earning
potential of the children and are worth quoting in full: [26b]

Sir,

I beg leave in this manner to communicate to
you and the managers of St Cuthbert's Charity
Workhouse such information as some of them
seemed to wish for with regard to the children
bound by them in 1790 as apprentices to Mr Dale,
and whose term of engagement is now on the point
of expiring.

They were in all 41 in number of whom 31
are still at Lanark, 9 having run away or been
carried off by their parents & one only is dead. The
31 who remain consist of 15 boys and 16 girls and
may in point of age be divided into three classes.

		Boys	Girls
The first may be about 15 years of age.			
Of these there are		2 &	4
second	13 to 14	8	9
third	11 to 12	5	3

It will be satisfactory to the Managers considering the state of their education when they went

to Lanark, to be informed that excepting four, the children can all read with considerable propriety. 19 have for some time been learning to write in which some of them have made considerable proficiency; a few of the boys have begun to learn figures and some of the girls to learn the use of the needle.

A number of them propose of their own accord, to continue some time longer in Mr Dale's service. Others wish previously to see and consult with their friends. And the rest say they wish to go to other trades, and private service.

In the second and third classes there are 13 who have no parents and being under the age of . . . . stand more in need of the attention of the Managers. Some of those who propose to continue at Lanark wish to do so upon a different footing from what they have hitherto been on, by drawing weekly wages and supporting themselves. Those of the first class who alone are capable of doing this with any propriety might in this way earn 3/6 per week. Were they or the others to continue on the same footing as they now are on, an additional allowance in money over and above their maintenance, cloathing and schooling, could be afforded them. To those of the first class, this would be about 13/- p. annum, to the 2nd, 10/- p. annum, and to the third 20/- for two years.

If the Managers approve of these terms and any new engagements follow either from their advice or the inclinations of the children themselves, they will readily see that from the age of the children their concurrence will be necessary to render the engagements valid.

> I am respectfully Sir
> Your vr. obdt. Humble Servant
> (signed) HUGH DICK **26b**

This system of frequent assessment and rewarding indicates that Dale was not just throwing books at children in the vague hope that they might learn a little. Here was a structured and progressive system of basic education, (i.e. progressing in difficulty) employing recognised teachers and small rewards for the pupils (and teachers) who succeeded.

Apart from these night 'schools', there were two day 'schools' (i.e. classes) run along the same lines. Thus far, nobody, except *possibly* Gillespie in Woodside, had provided a day school for the under sixes in a factory community. These day schools, as well as the evening ones, were free, except for the provision of one's own book. They had to be free for the pauper children of course, since they were not paid for their work in the factory, but given food, clothing and so on in lieu.

Once a pupil reached the top class, his evening class would consist of more writing than reading, with some time devoted to arithmetic, and sewing for the girls. Dale reports in 1796 that 12 boys and 12 girls had reached this stage from the class of 80.[26]

This instruction went on for four years for the children residing in the village of New Lanark. For the children in Number Four Mill, this could vary from 4—7 years, depending on their age on arrival from the workhouse, "or generally until they have completed their 15th year." [27] Thus, the pauper's bound apprenticeship at New Lanark was quite a bit longer than that of the village children, and it must be borne in mind that more profit could presumably be made from employing a pauper child for seven years without pay than from employing a village child for four years with pay. (Offset against this is the cost of board and lodging, but I suspect that the profit would still be there.)

Dale took care to ensure that living conditions were as humane as the late 18th Century would allow. The apprentice children slept 3 to a bed, 50—75 to a room, in six rooms allocated for this purpose. (This totals to more than the 175 mentioned in the *Old Statistical Account*, but the increase is verified in Dale's letter.)

One physician who visited in 1792 noted:

"Cleanliness, health and order pervaded the whole
manufactory. The children looked cheerful and
happy with rosy cheeks and chubby countenances,
and I found a variety of excellent regulations
established for health, morals and knowledge." [27b]

Hygiene was very important at this time, as the city of
Glasgow suffered a prolonged epidemic of smallpox from 1787–
91.[28] Even after this date, the deaths from this disease ran into
hundreds each year in Glasgow alone. Typhus fever was the other
major scourge. (Although cholera is mentioned, it did not reach
epidemic proportions until the late 1820's.) [29]

Dale makes no mention of cholera or smallpox by name,
but he does mention "typhus fevers" which had been in the
village, and had appeared in the paupers' lodgings some years
before, although he is proud of his success in keeping his place
clean and free from disease. From 1792–95, only 9 deaths
occurred.[30] To prevent the spread of disease, Dale ensured that:

"The ceilings and walls of the apartments are white-
washed twice a year with hot lime and the floors
washed with scalding water and sand . . . The bedrooms are carefully swept and the windows thrown
open every morning." [31]

Clothing was provided and this was made, not surprisingly,
from cotton. Each boy and girl was given two suits, one being
washed every fortnight, and in winter the suits were made from
wool. In fact, Dale had provided a type of uniform from the
earliest days of the village.

"When the building commenced, Mr Dale procured
a number of boys whom he equipped in complete
dress of brown cloth, with red collars to their coats
and sent them to Cromford to receive instruction
in the cotton spinning." [31b]

Both boys and girls had complete dress suits for Sundays. "Linens" (underclothes) were changed once a week.

Should these precautions against fevers still prove insufficient, the remedy was:

" . . . the immediate withdrawal of the sick to a detached part of the house, and frequent sprinkling and fumigating of the bedrooms with vinegar." [31]

Dale reports that the health of his pauper employees was good. The death rate was low and "the workers, when too big for spinning, are as stout and robust as others." [32]

Nevertheless, it seems clear from a letter to Mr Richardson of the Charity Workhouse in Edinburgh that Dale was certainly aware of this problem and did his best to ensure that as many as possible were retained at New Lanark, if they so wished. Dale felt that, in some cases, the period of indenture was too brief and that the children would be too young to find employment. The solution was obvious.

Mr Richard Richardson (Copy) Glasgow, 7 Sept. 1790

Sir,

". . . And with regard to the question whether I think the Children can get a tolerable subsistence when their indentures expire either at my work or at similar manufactures — the only doubt that remains in my mind is the age of the children when the indentures expire as the greatest part of them will be too young to make a judicious choice for themselves & also for taking the management of any branch of the business. Were the Managers to extend the term of their indentures for 5 or 6 years I think I can promise to put them all in a way of gaining their bread. The Girls might all continue in the Miln & receive such wages as grown up women get — a number of the boys might remain in the Mill — others might be taught to work on the loom and those who were stout might be taught to spin either on mule or common Jennies — those that chose to go to the loom or to spin on Jennies behoved to enter into a new indenture but I would owe them journeyman wages — in this way I think I could provide for all the children that the Town may send out from time to time and if I am spared in life might have the pleasure of introducing the well behaved among them to such employment as to enable (?) them not only to provide for themselves but to be useful to others.

I am &c

DAVID DALE   **32b**

Humane the conditions certainly were, but Dale could not possibly keep all of the children employed in the mills when their apprenticeships ran out. Some boys would be kept on as weavers, mechanics, masons, etc., but most of them went on elsewhere as spinners or weavers. The spinning system of carding, twisting and reeling was better suited to female employees:

"Were they disposed to continue at the mills, these afford abundant employment for them at reeling, picking etc."[32]

Dale explains the situation thus:

"The male part of them are fit for any trade. A great many since the commencement of the war have gone into the army and navy, and others are occasionally going away as apprentices to smiths and joiners etc., but especially to weavers; for which trade, from the expertness they acquire when handling yarn, they are particularly well fitted, and of course are taken as apprentices on better terms."[32]

By modern standards, the living conditions, educational
provision and terms of employment may appear primitive, but at
the time they were ahead of anything being offered elsewhere. I
can find no evidence to suggest that any other mill owner was
providing as much for his child labourers as Dale was. I have
suggested that at Cromford, Belper and Milford there were established "communities" with houses, markets and Sunday Schools,
and it may be that Dale's community was modelled on these.
Similarly, Gillespie's school may have been established in Glasgow,
but there is no evidence to indicate that any other child employees in Scotland were as well provided for as Dale's were. He
was justifiably proud of his scheme:

> "And when it is considered that the greater part of
> the children who are in the boarding house consists
> of destitute orphans, children abandoned by their
> parents . . . and many who know not who were their
> parents . . . it gives me great pleasure to say, that by
> proper management and attention, much *good* instead
> of evil may be done at cotton mills. For I am
> warranted in affirming that many now have stout,
> healthy bodies and are of decent behaviour who in all
> probability would have been languishing with disease
> and pests to society had they not been employed at
> Lanark cotton mills." [33]

New Lanark, of course, was Dale's biggest mill, owned entirely by himself, and was well-known, but it is interesting to in-
vestigate whether the systematised schooling to be found at New
Lanark was also established at the sites of some of his other
business ventures, such as Catrine and Blantyre.

At Catrine, which was established in 1786, it is difficult to
say for sure that it was Dale who caused the school to be built,
but it is not too far-fetched to suggest that it was. At New Lanark
(and a few months later at Blantyre, as I will argue) a school had
been provided at his own expense. These schools were not,

strictly speaking, necessary to the running of the mills, yet he had taken a fair amount of time, trouble and expense to provide them. It is possible that in a new venture at Catrine, starting from scratch, he would wish a school to be built, and it may be a hint that, in describing the school, the minister makes no reference to Mr Alexander, Dale's partner, but to "the company". None of this can be proved from the evidence available. It is enough to note that Dale was involved, in partnership with Alexander, in providing a school in Catrine. The parish minister noted that:

> "The company pay a very laudable attention to the morals and education of the youth. They have built a large school-room, and appointed a schoolmaster with an annual salary . . . and a free house . . . for which he teaches the children employed in the work from 7 to 9 o'clock in the evening." [34]

(One source states that this schooling was also available to adults, but there is no other evidence for this.) [35]

One wonders how many children would attend in the summer months when there was so much work to be done in the fields. (See Chapter 2.)

In addition to this full-time schoolmaster, one assistant was provided, earning £5, which was one third of the schoolmaster's annual salary. (The master stood to earn another £15 per annum from the day-school pupils.) The schoolmaster taught during the day to the under nines:

> "Children are not admitted into work under nine years old and they all lodge with their parents and friends. It is but justice to add that both young and old enjoy uniformly good health." [36]

The master's assistant was employed during the day in the twist mill as an under clerk. On Sundays, master and assistant met the children, catechised them and conducted them to church.

(There was a Chapel of Ease, "esteemed a great ornament to the place", built in 1792, supported by Alexander and local subscription. This has survived and is now the Parish Church in Catrine.)

Thus the factory school in Catrine was similar to the one at New Lanark in a number of ways, e.g. day schooling, evening school from 7–9 p.m., a combination of master and part-time assistant, and Sunday meetings in the school. However, one or two important differences must be borne in mind: the day school charged all the pupils for instruction; the pupils were aged up to 9 not 6 as at New Lanark; and they were not pauper children or bound apprentices obtained from an overseer. Also, the school seems to have been on a smaller scale, since only one master and one assistant were employed, which suggests that the subjects offered for study would be more limited than at New Lanark. This would seem to be quite natural, as the spinning at Catrine was on a much smaller scale than at New Lanark.

Exactly where this "large school-room" was in Catrine is difficult to ascertain. The map on page 26 does not show it as a separate building, but nothing definite can be read into this, given the crude nature of the map. It is also possible that it was situated in one of the five storeys or attics of the mill. (This is also a problem at New Lanark. The *Old Statistical Account* suggests that Number Four Mill could have been the school-room as well as the sleeping area, but this is not certain. The only other building where such numbers could have been accommodated was New Buildings, but it is also possible, given the high ceiling and the position of ventilation holes, that this was the dining area.)

In Catrine, the exact location is of no great importance, since I can find no other information regarding class size or subjects and mode of instruction.

As noted in Chapter 2, the works were sold to James Finlay & Co. in 1801 with Buchanan as manager. It is interesting to find that some fifteen years later, Buchanan states that production etc. had increased, but is a little vague about the provision of schooling. He states that "we have three schools at present, I think, in the village,"[37] and that "one of these schoolmasters is paid by the company to teach for one hour each day after work and on Sundays."[37] It is difficult to know exactly what this means. It is possible that "we" refers to the Catrine people, which would imply that only one school was attached to the factory, in which case the incidence of schooling had decreased since the time of Dale and Alexander, — only two hours' instruction being given and no assistants mentioned. If the "we" refers to James Finlay & Co., then of course the incidence of schooling had increased. Given that Buchanan could be precise about the hours and salary of the company schoolmaster but is unsure about the number of other schools, I suspect that the "we" refers to the Catrine people, but I can find no concrete evidence to back up this interpretation.

Dale's other business venture which also spawned a school was the Blantyre Cotton Mill. According to Cullen,[38] Dale's association with MacIntosh and the resulting interest in dyeing led Dale to establish Blantyre in 1787. This was sold in 1792 to James Monteith, and Cullen argues that it was Monteith who provided schooling for the children.[39] However, the Old Statistical Account figures for 1791 (i.e. when Dale still owned Blantyre' show that 60 "Barracks children" were employed in the mill and were fed, clothed, lodged and educated by the mill owner. The Old Statistical Account notes:

> "These children are in general orphans between 8 and 12 years of age. They are generally bound to the work by their relations for a few years; and are fed, clothed and lodged by the proprietor of the mill. He has a schoolmaster employed in teaching them in their spare hours; a surgeon to attend them when sick; and much praise is due to such a guardian of youth for his attention both to their health and education."[40]

Assuming this was written, as stated by the minister, in 1791, it proves that Dale had established a similar system to that of New Lanark (although no mention is made of day schools) with pauper children taught, fed, lodged etc. and a community established round the mill:

> "A considerable village is now built, for the accommodation of the people employed at this work, where formerly there was not a single house." [41]

Since this volume of the *Old Statistical Account* was published in 1792 (the year Blantyre was sold), it is unlikely that the report of the children's education was written in that year. Even if it had been, it is even more unlikely that Monteith bought the mill, established a schoolmaster and a system of feeding, clothing and lodging and had houses built, all in time for inclusion in the *Old Statistical Account* published that year. Thus the evidence, such as it is, points to Dale as the provider of such a system between the years 1787–92.

Hence the system of schooling which began at New Lanark in 1786 re-appeared, with slight variations, at Catrine in 1786–7 and Blantyre in 1787. Catrine and Blantyre do not seem to have been as extensive as New Lanark, or at least less has been written about them, but the fact remains that Dale's concern for his child employees was not confined to one factory only.

References and Notes

1   Report of the Minutes of Evidence of the Select Committee on the State of Children Employed in the Manufactories of the United Kingdom, 1816, pp. 8-9.

2   Ibid., pp. 278-80.

3   R.S. Fitton & A.P. Wadsworth, *The Strutts & the Arkwrights 1758-1830*, Manchester University Press, 1958, p. 102.

4   *Derby Mercury*, 25th August 1785, cited in Fitton & Wadsworth, op. cit., p. 102.

5   *Old Statistical Account*, Vol XII, p. 122.
6   Ibid., p. 116.
7   J. Simon, Was there a'' Charity School Movement?'' in B. Simon
    (Ed.), *Education in Leicestershire 1540-1940*, Leicester
    University Press, 1968.
8   *Old Statistical Account*, Vol XV, p. 36.
9   Ibid., p. 36.
10 According to Fitton & Wadsworth, op. cit., pp. 104-7, there is no
    evidence to suggest that Arkwright used parish apprentices, ''though
    they may have taken individual apprentices from overseers''. This
    seems to be based on newspaper articles of the time which
    advertised jobs for large families and made no mention of parish
    apprentices.   Also, Arkwright could draw on families of lead
    miners in the area.   There is still, however, the possibility that
    parish apprentices were used in addition to the others.
11 'Alfred' (S. Kydd), *The History of the Factory Movement From
    the Year 1802 to the Enactment of the Ten Hours Bill in 1847*,
    London, 1857, Vol. II, pp. 116-20.
12 Regulations of the Town's Hospital with the Original Constitution
    of the House, Glasgow, 1844.
13 'Alfred' (S. Kydd), op. cit., pp. 116-20.
14 *Old Statistical Account*, Vol. XV, p. 38.
15 T. Garnett, *Observations on a Tour t hrough t he Highlands*,
    London 1800, Vol. II, p. 234.
16 Dale's answer to 13 questions posed by T.B. Bayley of the Man-
    chester Board of Health. The full text of these answers is in A.
    Brown, *History of Glasgow*, Glasgow, 1797, Bk. 3, pp. 231-9.
    N.B. There is an extract of these answers in S.E. Maltby, *Man-
    chester and the Movement for National Elementary Education
    1800-1870, Manchester, 1918.*
17 *Old Statistical Account*, Vol. XV, p. 38.
18 Ibid., p. 40.
19 'Chronicle' in *Annual Register* 1792, London, 1799, p. 27.
20 T. Garnett, op. cit. Garnett says he gets his information from the
    Old Statistical Account and J. McNayr's Guide from Glasgow to
    the Highlands of Scotland, but McNayr quotes 16 teachers in 1797.
    This is made more confusing by T. Bernard in The Reports of the
    Society for Bettering the Condition of the Poor (1800), when he
    quotes 16 teachers and says he is indebted to Garnett for the infor-
    mation.

21   Garnett, op. cit., p. 235.
22   Fitton & Wadsworth, op. cit., p. 103.
23   J. Cleland, *Annals of Glasgow*, Glasgow 1817. pp. 195 ff.
24   Ibid.
25   Dale's reply to Bayley's letter (see Ref. 16) in A. Brown, op. cit., p. 233. "Schools" here refers to what we would call "classes".
26   A. Brown, op. cit., p. 234.
26b Hugh Dick, Manager at New Lanark, to the Managers of St Cuthbert's Charity Workhouse, 1795. Provided by Lorna Davidson at New Lanark.
27   Ibid., p. 235.
27b Letter from James Currie. I am indebted to Dr E. Royle of York University for this information.
28   J. Glaister, *Epidemic History of Glasgow 1783-1883*, Glasgow, 1886.
29   Ibid.
30   A. Brown, op. cit., p. 236-7.
31   Ibid., p. 236.
31b *Lanark, the Burgh and Its Councils 1469-1880.* A.D. Robertson.
32   A. Brown, op. cit., p. 239.
32b I am indebted to Lorna Davidson, Education Officer at New Lanark for providing me with a copy of this letter.
33   Extract from Dale's letter to T.B. Bayley in S.E. Maltby, op. cit., Appendix IV, p. 124.
34   *Old Statistical Account*, Vol XX, p. 180 ff.
35   *James Finlay & Co. Manufacturers & East India Merchants 1750-1950*, Glasgow 1954, pp. 56-7.
36   *Old Statistical Account*, Vol. XX, op. cit.
37   Reports of the Minutes of Evidence etc., op. cit., p. 10.
38   A. Cullen, *Adventures in Socialism*, Glasgow, J. Smith, 1910, p. 10.
39   Ibid., p. 11-12.
40   *Old Statistical Account*, Vol II, p. 216.
41   Ibid., p. 217.

PHILANTHROPY

It is extremely difficult to separate Dale's provision of schooling from his philanthropy, because in many ways they are one and the same thing. As I have already argued, there was no need to provide extensive schooling for his children. Nor was it, strictly speaking, necessary to provide comfortable, well-aired living quarters, good food and reasonable hours of work. Why then did he do it? To say that it was merely part of his religious or philanthropic nature is to ignore his shrewdness in business matters. I do not believe that it is ever possible to define someone's 'motives' for doing good to others. It is questionable also whether someone should be called a philanthropist who gives everything away and becomes a pauper, dependent on other people's 'philanthropy'. Dale was not like this, but the question still remains: "how much or how little do I have to give away to be called a philanthropist? "

Dale's religion, of course, had a great deal to do with his 'philanthropy', as I shall show in the next chapter, and this religion has to be borne in mind in any consideration of his business ventures. The idea that Dale was simply a rich merchant who gave his money to deserving causes has to be avoided. Certainly, he was more than sympathetic to requests from Dempster to help the unfortunate Highlanders in Spinningdale, and once again at New Lanark when a boat was shipwrecked. It is true also that he paid his workers' wages when the first mill was burned down. However, it must be remembered that Spinningdale was also a (small-scale) business partnership. The shipwreck was fortunate in that it provided workers for New Lanark at a time when most of the local people were against this form of employment, which also helps to explain why Dale paid their wages after the fire. His donations to the British and Foreign Bible Society were plentiful, but this is hardly surprising. Surely a rich Christian with such an evangelical spirit as Dale could be counted on for financial support?

Similarly, Dale was not just a businessman. He was a figure with some social standing in the community, and gestures of a philanthropic nature were bound to enhance this status. Having said that, I do not believe that he was some kind of wheeler-dealer do-gooder: I merely wish to point out the pitfalls of any attempt to see him as a rich man who gave his money away without good reason.

In the list of Directors of the Town's Hospital dated 14th November 1787, the names of Dale and Moncrieff appear for the first time. [1] The Town's Hospital was a charity workhouse established in 1733. To this institution came those people who were too old or sick to work (or beg), and the children were designated as paupers. They were fed. clothed, boarded and put to work if they were fit. A contemporary document records the income of the hospital for the year to June 1796 as £2359-8s-1¼d.[2] The bulk of the income came from Assessment and subscriptions from the Town Council, Merchants' House, Trades House and General Session. Dale by 1787 was a member of the Trades House and a fully matriculated member of the Merchants' House, as was Moncrieff by 1788. Thus it was that Dale was elected on to the Board of Directors of the Town's Hospital. (Each of the above institutions elected a number of Directors.)

Had Dale been merely a Director of the Hospital, he would have been required to meet there once a year, as a member of the "Yearly Committee". There the Directors would hear reports from the Preceptor (Overseer) on the running of the Hospital, the staffing situation, accounts and so on. However, as a contemporary list shows,[3] Dale was also a member of the Manufacturing Committee which, as far as I can gather from the minutes, met once a month. As far as I can discover, no real study has yet been made of the daily running of the Town's Hospital or Dale's involvement in it. Obviously this is too large an area to study in depth here, but I would like to take a closer look at it in an attempt to understand Dale's function as a Director.

In the "Rules relating to Overseers, viz. the Master and Mistress of the House", [4] the overseers are charged with keeping an accurate register of names, ages, length of residence, and, where appropriate, time of death for each of the inmates. They also had to keep accounts such as the one illustrated so that these might be inspected by the Directors. They had to supervise the medical inspection of each new inmate and were not allowed to receive any person who had not been recommended by the Directors. They were also responsible for the foodstuffs and for ensuring that those fit enough to work did so. They were assisted by a Clerk (a kind of book-keeper/Minutes Secretary), a surgeon, nurses, cooks and a schoolmaster, each having a set of rules and regulations to follow.

The work done by the inmates came to include by 1782 the manufacture of thread lace. According to the Minutes:

> "Ten girls were bound apprentices to that business in the house who were put under the care of Mrs Sinclair, and some of the young women who had been instructed at Renfrew were employed to teach the girls." [5]

By 1784, 29 girls were employed at this work and by 1788 the profits from one year's lace manufacture totalled £211.14s.6d and Mrs Sinclair was commended. [6]   This description of the situation agrees with J. Cleland's account of working life in the Town's Hospital:

> "The young make bobbin lace and fill in fleece cards; the old spin, weave, make clothes, shoes, tease oakum etc." [7]

The work was supervised by someone with the title "Overseer of the Manufactures" (not to be confused with Overseer of

the House) whose job it was to "keep an account of all the raw
materials used and how they are disposed of", and to give the
Clerk the completed goods for sale. The Overseer of the Manufactures reported to the Monthly Committee of which Dale was a
member.

In fact, Dale was associated with the Town's Hospital until
1795 (when his name ceased to appear on the list of Directors) in
a number of capacities. He was on the Manufacturing Committee
until 1791, then again from 1792–4, but his status as Director on
the Yearly Committee had changed. From David Dale, Town
Councillor in 1787, he became Bailie Dale and chaired the meeting
in 1791 and again in 1794–5. (There is no mention of Moncrieff
after 1789 although he was elected a Bailie in 1790. He refused
to take the office and was fined £40 "for not accepting the office
of the youngest merchant Bailie.") [8]

Thus Dale would have a good deal of say in the running of
this charitable institution, particularly on the manufacturing side.
But it is too much to suggest that his work (and money) for the
Town's Hospital was entirely philanthropic, because it is already
known that his pauper employees at New Lanark came from the
Glasgow and Edinburgh workhouses. What better child employees
could he have had than ones which had been trained in the Town's
Hospital under his own supervision?

Evidence that the children were put out on apprenticeships
is supplied as early as 1733–4, and there is no reason to suppose
that the procedure would have altered by Dale's time:

> "When the Committee thinks any of the Boys suff-
> iciently educated, the Master of the Hospital is to
> enter into indentures for them in the name of the
> Directors, engaging for their service during seven years
> to any farmer, or tradesman who inclines to take
> them, and engages to supply them with food and
> clothing, and to teach them the Art or Trade: And
> in like manner, to indent for the girls for three years,
> when they go to common service, and for five years

when they are to be taught a trade." [9]

In 1742, the children were employed

" . . . in teazing (sic) and spinning of cotton, flax and
wool; the old men in picking of oakum, and wool-
combing; and the old women such of them as are not
fit to be nurses to the children, or to the sick, are employed in Spinning of Linen and woollen yarn." [10]

It is worth bearing in mind at this point that the Town's
Hospital "apprenticeship" system really worked on two levels.
Firstly, the children in the Hospital were taught practical skills
from an early age, as a form of 'pre'-apprenticeship in preparation
for the world outside. Secondly, when the children left, they
were bound to a specific 'trade' for a certain period, after which
they would become tradesmen or journeymen. Dale's "apprenticeship" system really only worked on one level. When he got
his child employees, he set them to work on a number of different
jobs, e.g. picking, mending and so on. At the end of their
"apprenticeship" there was no guarantee that all the children
would be classed as "tradesmen" or journeymen weavers.

Thus it was no accident that Dale was on the Manufacturing
Committee of the House. His experience was undisputed and as
the benevolent proprietor of New Lanark, he could ensure that
conditions were not too harsh in the manufacturing area at least.
He, in turn, would be able to employ some of the pauper children.

He could also bring to the Hospital some experience as an
educator, though it must be said that in 1787 New Lanark had
only been in operation for one year, and it is possible that Dale
took some of his ideas *from* the Town's Hospital rather than
giving them *to* it.

The children at the Hospital were taught (according to a
newspaper cutting of 1792) [11] how to set the teeth in woollen
and cotton cards. Those of "maturer age" were taught how to
work thread lace and tambour muslin under the inspection of

proper teachers, without interruption to their education.[11]

In this way they had practical instruction as well as "education" and it may be that, since Dale did not emulate this idea in his own schools, he actually requested that this should happen. There is, of course, no evidence for this line of approach, merely a hint that if Dale was going to employ some of these children as apprentices, it would be much better if they knew what they were about. The Town's Hospital had to teach children these skills if they were ever to have a chance of a job when they left. Dale did not have to spend time teaching them skills outside working hours (except for some sewing and knitting). That time was reserved for "education".

"Education" in the Town's Hospital was in the hands of the schoolmaster. Like the rest of the staff, he was bound by a set of rules and regulations which included divine worship every morning and evening, plus the blessing of all meals; four hours' teaching per day during November, December and January and six hours per day during the rest of the year. This teaching meant reading, writing and the five common rules of arithmetic "for such as have time and genius".[12] Also included was the catechising of all the inmates for two hours every Tuesday afternoon and on the Sabbath, in preparation for the divine worship which he was to conduct.

The Catechism was taught from books with misleading titles such as *A Collection of Words in our Assembly's Catechism in an Easy and Natural Order,* compiled for the use of the Town's Hospital in 1748. This consists of daunting lists of words arranged alphabetically and according to the number of syllables, a companion to the Catechism but with no explanation of its meaning.

This suggests that the teacher was in fact chaplain as well, and this is further hinted at in the Minutes of the Directors up until 1794. Mr Sommerville is mentioned as Chaplain of the House and teacher. By 1794, however, new candidates were being examined for this job and again the post is referred to as "chaplain and schoolmaster". (Bailie Dale was in the chair at this time.)

Dale's own school at New Lanark employed teachers, not chaplains, and while they had to catechise the children and lead them to church in much the same way as above, their job was primarily concerned with instruction in the schoolroom, not from the pulpit.

It would appear then that the Town's Hospital's programme of instruction (which included spinning, tambouring etc.) was a fuller one than David Dale's. The Town's Hospital children were taught the three R's and given instruction which was supposed to help them find a job when they left. However, I would argue that Dale's New Lanark school had the edge on the Town's Hospital. He employed some 13 professional teachers to teach the children in classes, as against one "teacher" at the Town's Hospital. As for practical instruction, there could be none better than 'on the job' training, as it were, in Dale's own mills, in return for board and lodging. The children at New Lanark lived with their own kind, not with destitute adults and chronically sick or insane people as the Town's Hospital children did.

Similarly, there seems to have been a great hurry to dispose of these children from the Hospital:

"And as to such children, as are near the age at which they may be fit to learn mechanick employments, Care is taken to hasten their education, so as they may be timeously let out to apprenticeships: By which means the house will be eased of several each year, to make Room for others." [13]

Dale, however, was in no great hurry to dispose of his children. When their apprenticeship ran out, they had at least had the chance of a structured system of schooling, and those who came to him too young to work stood to gain even more.

Dale's involvement with the Town's Hospital is significant for a number of reasons. Firstly, it was a "philanthropic" gesture to involve his time and money in work for a charitable institution. Secondly, this philanthropy has to be tempered with the fact that

the Town's Hospital provided a pool of pauper employment from
which Dale could choose, (although some people might see his
employment of these children as a philanthropic gesture in itself).
Lastly, it is possible that Dale's experiences in the textile trade
would enhance the manufacturing process in the Hospital, and
thus improve the children's chances of employment.

Before moving on to Dale's involvement with the Royal
Infirmary, I should like to mention in passing two other philanthropic 'gestures' (for they were no more than that) of Dale's.

The first was reported in the *Glasgow Mercury* of 13th
March 1783 and is self-explanatory:

> "On Thursday and Friday last, Mr David Dale, mer-
> chant here, opened sales of a quantity of meal made
> from pease, which he has imported for the relief of
> the poor, at the low price of ten pence per peck. His
> generosity and benevolence upon the present occasion
> has been exemplary. He sold the bulk of the pease at
> the market price but gave five bolls to the hundred
> to societies who purchased that quantity. He pur-
> chased meal to supply the working poor of the Parish
> of Stewarton, his native place, selling it at one penny
> a peck below what it cost him. The humane reader
> will feel pleasure in being informed of the liberality
> of this worthy citizen, whose private charities are not
> outdone by the most opulent of fortunes."

The second gesture was in 1790, when he was made an
annual Director of the newly-formed Glasgow Humane Society.
The Society's aim then (as now) was "to recover to life persons
apparently drowned." According to the Minutes of the first
meeting,[14] anyone who gave a yearly subscription of one guinea
would be eligible to be a Director, or if any public body (e.g.
Town Council, Merchants' House) were to contribute £10, the
head of each society would be made a Director. Since Dale was
not yet the 'head' of any of the public bodies, he must have been

there in a personal capacity. He did, after all, live very near the banks of the Clyde. The sum of one guinea would hardly break his bank. After all, he spent much more when he sent the food boat north (see p. 30) and also during his involvement with Spinningdale. However, it is a distinct possibility that he helped to make up the "residue of the funds" [15] to begin with. There was no return for his money or time, except perhaps in terms of social recognition, so this appears as a genuinely charitable gesture.

Neither was there any immediate return in his involvement with the Royal Infirmary. The money for this institution was raised partly from public subscription and partly from the Magistrates and Town Council. The Infirmary was intended, according to the Burgh records:

" . . . for the reception of indigent persons under bodily distress in the west of Scotland and for establishing a fund towards its permanent support, and as this charitable scheme is of such importance . . . it is hoped the magistrates and Council will take it under their care and protection." [16]

The magistrates (of whom Dale was one by this time, 1791) and Council were sympathetic and gave £500 towards building costs. [17] When the Charter was granted, Dale, along with Scott Moncrieff and others (surgeons, lawyers, professors, an M.P.) was entrusted with "the management and direction of the whole affairs of the said Corporation, from the date of this Charter" [18] for a period of one year. The Abstract on the following page shows how this new Infirmary was to be managed, [18] and the next illustration (page 87) shows the very first list of managers with Dale's name included but not Moncrieff's. The Infirmary was opened in December 1795.

The year 1795 was in fact the only year in which Dale was a Manager or Director of the Infirmary, but a close look at the list of subscribers shows that he gave money every year until 1806,

ABSTRACT

of the

CHARTER OF THE GLASGOW ROYAL INFIRMARY

By the Charter, the management of the affairs of the Infirmary is vested in 25 Managers or Directors, of which numbers, seven, from their office, are Managers without election or nomination, viz.

> The Lord Provost of Glasgow,
> The Member of Parliament for the City,
> The Dean of Guild,
> The Deacon Convener,
> The Professor of Medicine,
> The Professor of Anatomy,
> The President of the Faculty of Physicians and Surgeons,
>> Eighteen Managers annually elected, viz.
> One by the Magistrates and Council,
> One by the Merchants' House,
> One by the Trades' House
> One by the Faculty of the College,
> One by the Ministers of Glasgow,
> Three by the Faculty of Physicians and Surgeons,
> Ten, by Contributors of £10 or more, and Subscribers of £2.2s. annually, or more, and by the Preses's or Heads of Societies or Bodies of men who have contributed £50 or more, or who have subscribed annually £5.5s. or more.

A REPORT

OF THE ROYAL INFIRMARY OF GLASGOW, FROM ITS FIRST ESTABLISH-
MENT 8th. DECEMBER 1794, TILL 1ft. JANUARY 1796,

FOR THE YEAR 1795.

ROYAL *Infirmary* GLASGOW.

LIST OF MANAGERS, 1795.

John Dunlop, Efq. Lord Provoft,
William M'Dowall, Efq. M. P.
John Laurie, Efq. Dean of Guild,
William Auchinclofs, Efq. Deacon Convener,
Dr. Tho. Charles Hope, Profeffor of Medicine,
Dr. James Jeffray, Profeffor of Anatomy and
    Botany,
Dr. Cleghorn, in place of the Prefident of the
    Faculty of Phyficians and Surgeons,
Dr. Wright,
Dr. Taylor,
Meffrs. David Dale,
        Robert Waddel,
        Archibald Grahame,

Meffrs. John Stirling,
        Henry Riddel,
        John Buchanan,
        John Alfton,
        Gilbert Hamilton,
        Walter Ewing M'Lae,
        William Wardlaw,
        William Couper,
        John Swanfton,
        James Monteith,
        Archibald Smith,
        John Gordon.
        Profeffor Jardine,

the year of his death. His initial contribution in 1795 was £200 [19] and he is named in the same year as an annual subscriber of two guineas. (He raised this to five guineas in 1797.) This sum of £200 was a great deal of money in those days. It was the largest donation given by any one person, and was only surpassed by Institutions, e.g. the Merchants' House (£400) and the city of Glasgow (£500). Dale's sometime partners, Alexander, MacIntosh and Moncrieff, gave £50, £50 and 10 guineas respectively, Moncrieff like Dale agreeing to pay an annual subscription of two guineas.

Also in 1795 a donation of £50 was received from "the Work people at the Cotton mills near Lanark, under the name of the Benevolent Society there."[19] I have been unable to discover anything about this Benevolent Society at New Lanark, and I am left to guess at where this £50 came from (although Dr Currie does mention a bank or savings scheme in the village).[19b] It is possible that Dale encouraged his workers to donate something. He could have done this from the pulpit in the meeting-house. It is also possible that he deducted a small sum from the wages to 'pool' as a Benevolent Fund. Alternatively, he may simply have donated £50 of his own money and requested that it be entered under the name of the Benevolent Society. Whatever the case, a total of £250 came from Dale and New Lanark in 1795.

I mentioned earlier that there was no material return for his money, and there is no doubt that his donations were more than generous and would be put to good use in helping the sick people of Glasgow. While I would not detract in any way from Dale's generosity throughout his life, there is another side to his donations to the Royal Infirmary which has to be considered in any attempt to get a balanced picture of the man.

According to the regulations for admission of patients, as enacted by the General Court in January 1794, it could be argued that Dale, by contributing £200 and (after 1795) 5 guineas per year, had in fact taken out a kind of private medical insurance which would guarantee that he and his four daughters would be well placed if they ever had to be taken to the Infirmary, i.e. they would not have to wait for medical attention.[20]Since Dale was the biggest single 'Contributor', he or any of his family (and his servants) would be top of the waiting list. This might also help to explain a rather mysterious entry in the list of subscribers: "David Dale for four ladies, 8 guineas," which appeared for a number of years. In the event of his sudden death, his daughters would each have had their subscriptions paid for the rest of that year. In 1807, after his death, the daughters continued the subscriptions under their own names — "Miss Dale, Miss Mary, Miss Margaret, Miss Julia."

However, the Infirmary was a charitable institution established to help the sick and diseased poor, so neither Dale nor his family would actually qualify for treatment in the hospital, although his retired workers might. Also, given the nature of the place in those days, it is extremely unlikely that any wealthy middle-class merchant would wish to be treated there. [21] What is more probable is that Dale's association with the Infirmary would enable him to call on the services of the doctors who worked there part-time. He could certainly afford to pay their fees, and thus, to a certain extent, he was "insured" against ill health, although of course two of his children died at an early age.

I have no evidence to 'prove' any of this, and indeed, as I have already argued, one cannot 'prove' anyone else's motives for doing something. It could be argued that Dale simply gave his money to the Infirmary because it was a deserving cause, like the Bridewell perhaps (to which he gave £250 in 1799).[22] I believe, however, that in order to establish a more balanced and realistic view of events, several possibilities must be pursued, not just the 'charity' one. Hence my suggestions above.

References and Notes

1   Glasgow Town's Hospital Minutes 1732-1816, Mitchell Library MSS.
2   "Income and Expenditure of the Town's Hospital 1796", Glasgow University Library Special Collections.

3   Town's Hospital Minutes, op. cit., 14th November 1787.
4   "Regulations of the Town's Hospital 1733-4". These remained
     unchanged until the 19th century.
5   Town's Hospital Minutes, 17th February 1785 - refers to 1st
     January 1782.
6   Ibid., February 1788.
7   J. Cleland, *Annals of Glasgow*, Glasgow, 1817, p. 202.
8   Extracts from the Records of the Burgh of Glasgow, Glasgow,
     1913, Vol. III, 1781-1795, p. 379.
9   Regulations of the Town's Hospital, op. cit., p. 28.
10   *A Short Account of the Town's Hospital i n Glasgow with the
     Abstracts of the Expenses for the First Three Years*, 4th Edition,
     Edinburgh, 1742.
11   Included in "Income and Expenditure", see Reference 2.
12   Regulations of the Town's Hospital, 1735.
13   *A Short Account . . .*, op. cit.
14   Minutes of the Glasgow Humane Society, 16th August 1790,
     Strathclyde Regional Archives.
15   Senex (R. Reid), *Old Glasgow and its Environs*, Glasgow, 1864,
     p. 207.
16   *Extracts from the Records of the Burgh of Glasgow*,   Glasgow,
     1913, Vol. III, 1781-1795, p. 210.
17   Ibid., p. 222.
18   Royal Infirmary Charter 1792, Mitchell Library.
19   Report of the Managers of the Royal Infirmary 1795,   Mitchell
     Library.
19b Letter from Dr Currie to Earl of Galloway, Dec. 1802. Provided
     by Dr Royle of York University.
20   Royal Infirmary Charter 1792, Mitchell Library.
21   I am indebted to Dr D. Dow, Greater Glasgow Health Board
     Archivist for this information. The Admission Registers show
     that from 1795, Dale recommended some 50 people for treat-
     ment at the Infirmary, most from Glasgow or Lanark, but some
     from as far afield as Campbeltown, Islay, Ireland. The most
     common complaints seem to have been chincough (whooping-
     cough), ulcers, fevers and sivvens (syphilis).
22   See Note 16 above. *Burgh Records*, Vol. III, p. 162.

EVANGELISM

Thus far, I have been concerned to review Dale's career as a successful businessman in 18th Century Glasgow and to consider how far the social and educational provision which he made for his workers was motivated by a fundamentally philanthropic nature. There is, however, one glaring omission from all this which makes any account of Dale's life quite incomplete. This side of David Dale was apparent before he was a rich man, existed during his extensive business career, and continued after his retirement until his death in 1806. I am referring of course to his religious beliefs and his lifelong work on their behalf.

It is one thing to say that Dale had strong religious beliefs, but quite another to call this evangelism. Yet I believe that he was an evangelist, i.e. he believed that it was his duty to spread the word as far as possible and to practise what he preached. His Christianity for him was not something aesthetic and part-time, but a firm set of convictions upon which to base his life. I would not push the case as far as some churchmen would like and argue that this Christianity was the sole inspiration for all of Dale's business, educational and philanthropic ventures, but its importance cannot be ignored in any assessment of his achievements.

According to Liddell's *Memoir*, [1] Dale's association with the church (that is the Presbyterian Church of Scotland at that time) began during his apprenticeship in Paisley. Apparently he "sought the company of religious people" and "attached himself to the evangelical party in the Established Church", the fellowship meetings being held during the evening in a private house. Of course it is quite possible that his connection with the church may have stemmed from a religious childhood, but I can find no evidence of William Dale's association with the church in Stewarton.

When Dale came to Glasgow in 1763, this religious con-
sciousness was continued in his association with the College
Church congregation for about five years until he was visited by
a Mr John Barclay (the future leader of an Independent sect
known as The Bereans).

During Dale's association with the Established Church, the
question of patronage came to the fore. What normally happened
was that the General Session up until 1764 had exercised the
right of patronage to all the town churches: they appointed the
ministers as they saw fit, and the Session was made up of elders
and ministers from the eight parishes within the city. However,
by 1764, this right was challenged by the magistrates and Town
Council. The case was taken to the Court of Session and "by a
decree of the court, the magistrates prevailed and were declared
patrons." [2]

The first vacancy was at Dale's church in the College Wynd
and the magistrates lost no time in exercising their new power,
promptly having the pulpit supplied with a minister of their own
choosing. According to Liddell:

> "This appointment gave great offence, not only to
> the parishioners, but to the citizens generally, who
> valued their religious privileges. Great dissatisfaction
> was evinced by the orthodox party in the Wynd con-
> gregation." [3]

One of the members of this "orthodox party" was David
Dale. Another was Archibald Paterson, the candlemaker who had
entered into partnership with Dale in the High Street. Dale,
Paterson, "Matthew Alexander and some others" [4] opened a subscription in an attempt to break away from the Wynd Church,
although this breakaway group was still part of the Established
Church and its Presbyterian principles (i.e. Presbytery controlling
the licensing and appointment of ministers).

Among them, this group managed to raise enough money to
build a new meeting-house in North Albion Street. This building

was named "The Chapel of the Scotch Presbyterian Society" but
was later changed to "The Chapel of Ease". Dale was a subscriber and voted for the first minister, a Mr Cruden. [5] Dale continued to be associated with this church until 1786 when John
Barclay appeared on the scene. Barclay's preaching, according to
Liddell

> " . . . had the effect of leading those individuals to a
> more thorough searching of the Scriptures for light
> and guidance, which ended in their gradually em-
> bracing Congregational principles in church govern-
> ment." [6]

Of course, by removing themselves from the College Church
over the question of patronage, Dale and the others would have
been open to Barclay's 'new' ideas on Congregationalism, but for
a better understanding of the situation, it is necessary to look
briefly at the rise of this notion of Congregationalism up to and
including 1769.

In a recent thesis on this subject, [7] D.B. Murray argues that
John Glas was the 'founding father' of the Independent Churches.
Glas was ordained in 1719 and published his views on the separate-
ness of the church from any civil authority in 1726. The General
Assembly, not surprisingly, suspended him two years later. Glas
fought this but in 1730 the Commission of the Assembly con-
firmed the Synod's ruling that he be suspended for "divisive and
schismatical courses in setting up his own meeting houses." [8]

Since Glas's principles had their foundation in the idea of
Independence anyway, it is hardly surprising that this deposition
seemed to have little effect. It did not stop him preaching and he
travelled the countryside propounding his ideas and appointing
men to preach these ideas in his absence. Thus it was that when
the Assembly offered him a reconciliation if he renounced his
Independent principles, he was able to refuse and carry on with
his preaching.

Glas's ideas lived on after his death, and the notion of an

Independent church based on Congregational principles found
favour with two ministers in Fife, James Smith of Newburn
Parish and Robert Ferrier of the neighbouring Largo Parish.
Smith had, by 1757, read some of Glas's own works, but in particular the Religious Tracts written by Glas's son-in-law. So influenced was Smith that he began writing his own views on
Independency. Ferrier had read Glas's works too and became ac-
quainted with Smith. They both resigned from the Presbyterian
Church on 17th August 1786 and began holding local meetings in
farm buildings.

In Glasgow at the same time John Barclay, himself a dis-
senting licentiate from the parish of Fettercairn, visited Dale and
the others. Why he chose to visit at all is unclear, but it is possible
that the magistrates' decision and the anger of the congregation
had reached Barclay, already sympathetic to the idea of an Independent church. According to the account in the General
Register of the Old Scotch Independent Church, it was Barclay
who persuaded Dale and the others to break with Presbyterianism
altogether:

> " . . . impressing strongly upon them the necessity of
> searching the Scriptures and judging from and being
> directed by them in these matters. Mr Dale and his
> friends by doing so were soon sensible that the
> Christian brotherhood and brotherly love, so much
> insisted on in the Scriptures . . . were incompatible
> with the systems they had hitherto been attached to." [9]

Consequently Dale, Paterson and the others left the Chapel
of Ease in 1768 and began to assemble every Sunday in a private
house until the end of that year, when the numbers reached 25
and a new meeting house was erected in Greyfriars Wynd. The
Old [10] Scotch Independents had their first church building. It
could seat 500 and was financed entirely, it seems, [11] by
Archibald Paterson. It became known as the "caunnel kirk"
because of Paterson's association with candle making.

By this time, Smith and Ferrier had published their views on the non-intervention of civil powers in church affairs and the congregation's power of censure and discipline, in a pamphlet entitled "The case of James Smith and Robert Ferrier truly represented and Defended".[12] They had managed to establish a meeting house at Balchristie in Fife where they "presided as elders". It must be stressed that until the year 1768, the rise of these two Independent Churches in Fife and Glasgow was quite separate and unconnected, but the publication of the pamphlet by Smith and Ferrier had brought them to the attention of the public and

> "the statements and doctrines in these publications being in accordance with the views of the Glasgow seceders, led to the opening of a correspondence between them which resulted in their union."[13]

The General Register [14] states that members of the Glasgow congregation actually visited Fife and prevailed on Ferrier to come to Glasgow to the new meeting house as an elder. ("Elder" to the Independents meant pastor or minister.) Ferrier agreed and Dale was unanimously elected to serve with him in 1769. Thus began Dale's lifelong task as a Christian pastor. The list[15] illustrated below shows Ferrier and Dale as the first elders:

33

List of Elders in the Church at Glasgow from 1768 ~~till 1800~~.

	appointed	
Robert Ferrier	1769	Left the Church from Glassite views
David Dale	1769	Died 17 Mar 1806, after a long & faithful ministry.
Robert Moncrieff	1774	Left the Church from Baptist views
William Cleland	1778	died 10 Dec 1801, after a long faithful ministry.
William Kelly	1800	died 15 June 1839 at Row near Helensburgh
David Hill	1801	Resigned the office 1810. Went to Edin' 1811.

The fact that Dale was not a trained, licensed preacher aroused anger amongst many Glasgow church-goers. Dale is reported [16] to have been booed and jostled in the streets and sometimes had to take refuge in a sympathiser's house. As a further indication of their dislike, the mob often packed "the caunnel kirk" to create a noisy scene during the service. Even Ferrier, who was licensed to preach, was subjected to shouts and insults, but "more personal respect was shown to him than to Mr Dale." [17]

Exactly how long this went on is not clear. Certainly Dale put up with it for some years and the mob who had derided him in 1769 later cheered him on his walk through the town as a magistrate. (It was the custom for the magistrates, in full ceremonial dress, to walk to church at times during the year. They were escorted by city officers. Since Dale was not a member of the Established church, he refused to go there and so he was escorted to his own church.)

It will be noted from the list of elders that Ferrier left the Independents after a while because of his strict Glassite views. Robert Moncrieff (an apothecary, not to be confused with Robert Scott Moncrieff) left to become a Baptist. This merely reflects the growing tide of Independent church movements at the time. There were the Bereans (named after a Biblical town), Anabaptists, Glassites, Baptists and others. The Baptists, in particular, drew many away from Dale's congregation and even Mrs Dale left to join them. However,

"Nothing daunted, Mr Dale stuck to his colours, and though the church was reduced to a mere skeleton, yet by renewed exertions it soon recovered its wonted strength and numbers." [18]

So far, this account of Dale's involvement with the Independents has been largely historical. It is necessary now to attempt to relate some of the principles of the Old Scotch Independents to Dale's own life.

The members recognised no authority, civil or ecclesiastical,

other than the Bible. This meant not only that the magistrates
had no right to appoint ministers on the congregation's behalf,
but also that anyone could receive the call of God and could
preach if he fitted the Apostolic conditions in Scripture. This
meant not just a strong belief in God but active participation in
the work of preaching and converting. Thus they disapproved of
full-time ministers paid for this purpose. They had a plurality of
elders who could and would preach if required, as well as carrying
out the day to day work of the church.

It should be emphasised, however, that the Old Scotch Independents were not a group of messianic radicals out to re-
organise the social structure. Far from it. They seem to have
been an extremely conservative, pro-establishment sect. According to Brown's *Religious Denominations of Glasgow*,

> "they retain a strong bias for the doctrines of the
> national establishment, and consider they have suc-
> ceeded in clarifying and purifying them." [19]

Further:

> "Degeneracy from original principles, which has over-
> taken many, has not yet overtaken the Old Scotch
> Independents. They may not have progressed ac-
> cording to their advantages, but they have not retro-
> graded." [20]

In other words, it was a strictly conservative sect which saw
some of the trappings of Presbyterianism (e.g. the place of Com-
munion and the order of hymns) as Papist.

Nevertheless, their belief that those who had the talent to
preach ought to do so and their active Christianity made them
less introspective than is perhaps suggested above. They followed
a simple example from the Bible. Jesus and the Apostles taught
by word and example and used to the full what talents they had.
The Old Scotch Independents must do likewise. Indeed, not to

do so would be a sin, as exemplified in the Parable of the Talents. Further, according to Liddell, those who had the talents in the church "were not only at liberty but were bound to exercise them for the *good* of their fellow creatures." [21]

This helps to explain why Dale's Sundays were always spent preaching the word to different congregations, despite initial opposition to an 'unqualified' minister. He became "the first individual in the Kingdom who, as a layman, administered ministerial functions." [22] More importantly, the rest of the week was spent actively carrying out these principles. If talents had to be used, then what better way to do it than by using one's own talents to help others to discover theirs: in other words, by providing educational and moral training for young children?

The business side had its place in this scheme too. According to Brown, [23] one of the principles of the Old Scotch Independents was "personal election to grace". What I take this to mean is that a state of grace (to use a non-presbyterian term) can be achieved between man and God only if the man has lived by the Bible and has 'proved' himself by using any wealth, power or influence to do good in the world. It seems to be based on the Calvinistic idea of "an elect", which would certainly stress the importance of business and profit as a 'talent' to be fostered. I do not wish to confuse the issue of "an elect" with personal election, but it should be noted that the idea of personal election rather neatly avoids one of the central problems of Calvinist theory: how one becomes a member of the elect? (That is, is one chosen or is it 'earned' and which comes first?) Thus, while the notion of personal election avoids the problem in Calvinist theology, it retains the Calvinist emphasis on business and profit as respectable and desirable. Dale had an undeniable 'talent' for business and he used this talent to the full. When this is added to his educational and charitable work, it may be argued that he was, according to the principles of the Old Scotch Independents, well on his way to this state of "grace".

That Dale was able to withstand the initial mockery and derision of the public says much for his strength of faith and evangelical spirit. This is what inspired him to preach at Bridewell and in later life (a particularly busy time for him as a pastor and evangelist) to become involved in the British and Foreign Bible Society's efforts to translate the Bible into several languages, a a cause to which he donated large sums of money.

For someone with such intense beliefs, the whole of life must, as far as possible, be lived according to these beliefs. In a sermon given by Dale on 8th January 1792 [24] on the Biblical text Luke X, 42 (on "choosing the right thing") it may be seen how he interpreted the Scriptures for everyday living, and it is only a short step for us to relate this interpretation to his own life.

He notes that the Lord was always to be found doing good and that this was a duty for all:

> "Our minds should be convinced that every thing we
> do is present duty and in discharge of it we should
> aim at glorifying God and doing good to ourselves
> and others." [25]

Further:

> "Diligence in business matters is a duty; but in this
> and in all things, we should be 'fervent in spirit,
> serving the Lord', which cannot be the case if this
> duty is attended to at the expense of another more
> important."

On the question of salvation, Dale seems to have been particularly eloquent. This 'greatest of concerns' is spoken of at length. Indeed, in a letter to his father [26] (see following page) concerning the death of Dale's daughter, almost the entire space is devoted to the question of salvation and how this is a perennial, assured to all believers. This is important, since it suggests that Dale was concerned not only with 'doing good', but with actively encouraging religion and good deeds as a means towards salvation. The letter notes that all human concerns are trivial in

relation to salvation. Salvation can be found in God's word
(which is eternal, unlike humans) and he advises his father to
search the Scriptures for help in this matter. His father could
read: the children at New Lanark could not, so they were taught
how to. (Reading the Bible and "Salvation" are important
elements in Calvinist thought.)

My Dear Father

Glasgow 26th May 1783

*I am sorry to inform you that my youngest
daughter died the 17th Curr[t] of the Chincough. it becomes
me to say not my will but the will of the Lord be done
what is our life it is even as a vapour that continueth
a little & then vanisheth away. as mortals on the brink
of eternity we are called to hear & believe the Gospel of
Christ. now is the accepted time now is the day of
Salvation to day let us hear the voice of Christ. how
shall we escape if we neglect so great salvation.*

On money and wealth, Dale is quite explicit:

> "Riches are one great object. These frequently take
> to themselves wings and fly away; and though they
> should not, yet they profit not in the day of wrath.
> And if these are obtained by oppressing the poor, or
> withholding from the needy what his wants demand
> from us, the consequence is awful . . . your riches are
> corrupted." [27]

Dale's religious work and beliefs ought to indicate at least
some link between business, education and religion. It is im-

possible to *prove* that religion inspired and controlled his business life, but it was certainly a significant factor. Dr Ralph Wardlaw, famous Congregationalist and one-time Professor at the Theological Academy in Albion Street, while noting that Dale's life-style was not entirely in accordance with Christian moderation, seemed in no doubt that religion was the force behind all that Dale did. In an Obituary notice in *The Glasgow Herald* of March 1806, Wardlaw wrote:

> "Impelled by the all-powerful influence of that truth which he firmly believed and publicly taught . . . his ear was never shut to the cry of distress . . . every public institution which had for its object the alleviation of human misery in this world . . . received from him the most liberal support and encouragement." [28]

The editor of *The Evening Star* in London, who was originally from Glasgow, wrote:

> "His motive [in erecting the cotton mills] was to extend the means of employment for the labouring poor . . . and render them useful to their families and the community." [28]

I doubt whether Dale's *motive* for erecting mills and schools was solely and entirely religious, but religion was quite definitely a significant influence in his life as a businessman, employer and educator.

References and Notes

1   Andrew Liddell, *Memoir of David Dale Esq.*, Glasgow, 1854, p. 167. This biography is very inadequate on Dale's early life and business career, but it does give a reasonable account of his religious work.

2   *The Rise of the Congregational or Independent Churches in Scotland* in Old Scotch Independent Church General Register, Strathclyde Regional Archives, T.D. 420.

3   Liddell, op. citl., p. 168.

4   *Rise of the Congregational Churches* , op. cit., p. 27.

5   Liddell, op. cit., p. 168.

6   Ibid., p. 169.

7   D.B. Murray, *The Social and Religious Origins of Scottish non-Presbyterian Dissent from 1730-1800*, Ph.D. Thesis, St. Andrews 1976, Chapter 2, p. 37. I am indebted to Murray's thesis for much of the history of the Old Scotch Independents.

8   Murray, op. cit., p. 41.

9   *Rise of the Congregational Churches*, op. cit., p. 28.

10   The "Old" came many years later, to distinguish it from the more modern independent sects set up by people like Haldane and Ewing and the Inghamites in England, with whom the Old Scotch Independents joined forces in 1814.

11   Liddell, op. cit., p. 169.

12   Cited by D.B. Murray, op. cit., p. 50.

13   Liddell, op. cit., p. 169.

14   *Rise of the Congregational Churches*, op. cit. p. 28.

15   Ibid., p. 33.

16   J. Brown, *Religious Denominations of Glasgow*, Glasgow, 1860, Vol. I, p. 23.

17   Liddell, op. cit., p. 169.

18   J. Brown, op. cit., p. 24.

19   Ibid., p. 26.

20   Ibid., p. 28.

21   Liddell, op. cit., p. 169.

22   J. Brown, op. cit., p. 22.

23   Ibid., p. 26.

24   *Substance of a Discourse by David Dale*, January 1792, publication date unknown. In Glasgow University Library Euing Collection.

25   Ibid., p. 4.

26   Liddell, op. cit., Appendix. See Transcription on page 108.

27   *Substance of a Discourse*, op. cit., p. 7.

28   Liddell, op. cit., p. 176-7.

David Dale, from inauspicious beginnings in Stewarton, created a fortune for himself, gave employment and housing to thousands of people, and fed, clothed and educated hundreds of children who would almost certainly not have had such opportunities under any other owner at that time. Anecdotes about him stress how benevolent he was and how the sight of people in distress pained him and prompted him to put his hand in his pocket. Reports, particularly in Garnett, *The Society for Bettering the Conditions of the Poor*, and McNayr's *Guide*, emphasis how well fed, happy and healthy his young employees were because of the attention Dale gave to domestic conditions and to education, and these reports rejoice at his philanthropy.

In his declining years he was concerned that any new owner would continue this tradition:

> "I have been rather indifferent in my health for some time past and I wish much to retire from business but I am afraid that I will not get the works easily disposed of. I would not wish to dispose of them to any person that would not follow out the plan I have laid down for preserving the health and morals of the children." [1]

While it is my contention that Dale *was* genuinely concerned for his employees and for the education of the children (as witnessed especially at New Lanark and Blantyre) and that New Lanark was a 'model' establishment, I have tried to resist the temptation to see New Lanark as his only achievement. I have also tried to avoid giving a one-sided view of Dale as a benign old gentleman who simply gave sums of money to deserving causes.

He had many business ventures, and, after all, the factory community was not Dale's invention, nor was the idea of giving the children some form of education a new one. Arkwright, Strutt and Gillespie (and indeed others such as Greg and Oldknow) had their parts to play.

Dale did give his money to deserving causes, but he often received benefits in one way and another from these gestures. (For example, the Town's Hospital and the Royal Infirmary.) The benevolent Christian philanthropist view of Dale takes a knock from Andrew Liddell, who explains that the common practice of the time was to employ someone for a period of 10–12 years at a salary fixed at the commencement of employment. Dale followed this example, but when any such employee was promoted, Dale refused to increase his salary accordingly:

> " . . . nor in general would he allow the individual to leave until the end of the engagement, even when his doing so would have improved his circumstances. No doubt he acted in strict justice, but not with that generosity which his great benevolence would have led us to expect. His actings in these matters were considered by his best friends as rather sharp dealings." [1b]

Of the well clothed, lodged, fed and educated children at New Lanark, Robert Owen (never given to understatement) noted:

> " . . . Some of them became dwarfs in body and mind and some were deformed. Their labour throughout the day, and their education at night became so irksome that numbers of them continually ran away." [2]

Although Owen says that they were well clothed and so on, and were taught by the best instructors in the country, he accuses Dale of working them too hard in the mills and of "a strong sectarian influence which gave a marked and decided preference to one set of religious opinions over all others." [2] The New Lanark community, according to Owen, was stricken with "theft", "idleness and drunkenness", "falsehood" and "deception" and the people were "strongly experiencing the misery which these ever produce." [3]

Owen was comparing what he found with what he later managed to accomplish. Since his view of his accomplishments at New Lanark could hardly be described as modest, it would be natural for him to exaggerate about the conditions which existed before he took over, with the odd reference to Dale's charitable nature in order not to offend Caroline. Owen rarely gave credit where it was due (e.g. James Buchanan) unless he felt that it was due also to himself. Nevertheless, it cannot be denied that Dale's hours were long (remembering that Owen extended them for a while); that conditions were primitive; and that Dale was seldom there to ensure that his instructions were carried out. However, after considering the evidence, I would still argue that Owen owed Dale a tremendous debt, as this book has striven to prove.

Inspired by his religion and his natural business acumen, Dale must have worked at a prodigious pace throughout his life. The community at New Lanark did thrive, despite Owen's suggestions to the contrary, as did the ones at Blantyre and Catrine. The children were catered for in as charitable a way as the times allowed. There was no need, in strictly business terms, for him to provide schooling for the children. Others in the spinning business merely provided Sunday Schools if they felt that the morals of the children had to be catered for, and education meant catechising and Scripture reading. Not so David Dale: a combination of a brand of religion which emphasised the talents of the individual and salvation through work and belief in God, a kind of Calvinist approach to business through constant effort and expansion, and a vast amount of money with which to put his beliefs into practice, made the communities with which he was associated, particularly New Lanark, different from the others of the same period. At New Lanark, for which he will perhaps be most remembered, his ideas acquired their most tangible form, but his whole life was dedicated to business, religion, education and charity. He was truly "a bright luminary to Scotland."

References and Notes

1   Letter to Dr Currie, July 1798.
1b   A Liddell, *Memoir of David Dale Esq.*, Glasgow 1884, p. 175.
2   R. Owen, *A New View of Society*, London, 1813, pp. 13-19.
3   R. Owen, *A Statement Regarding the New Lanark Establishment*, Edinburgh, J. Moir, 1818, p. 5.

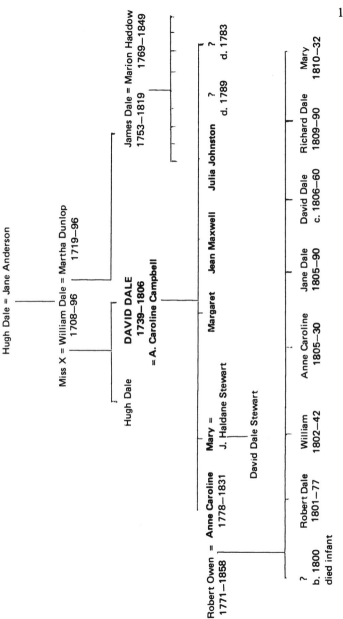

FAMILY TREE

Transcription of a letter written by Dale to his father after the death of his daughter in 1783 (retaining the original spelling)

Glasgow, 26th May 1783

Dear Father,

I am sorry to inform you that my youngest daughter died the 17th currt. of the Chincough. It becomes me to say not my will but the will of the Lord be done. What is our life? It is even as a vapour that continueth a little and then vanisheth away. As mortals on the brink of eternity we are called to hear and believe the Gospel of Christ. Now is the accepted time, now is the day of Salvation. Today let us hear the voice of Christ. How shall we escape if we neglect so great salvation? What is a man profited if he should gain the whole world & lose his own soul? Attention to the word of Christ is the one thing needfull. May you and I chuse the good part that shall never be taken from us. The Gospel reveals a righteousness which is allsuficient to save us, even the righteousness of Jesus Christ which he finished upon the cross. And it is by believing or giving credit to the testimony of God concerning the perfection of this righteousness that we come to the enjoyment of it. This believing is set in opposition to all our own working to become righteous. Hear and your soul shall live is the voice of God to those who are spending their labour for that which satisfieth not. Oh my dear Father, suffer me to Exhort you to search the Scriptures. There you will find that we are self destroyed sinners and that your help is on God. He laid our help upon one mighty to save, able to save to the utmost all that come unto God by him. When we think of the great importance of this salvation we have reason to be astonished at our own indifference about it. In a little time the triffles that now engage our attention will vanish like a dream. The earth & all that is therein shall be burnt up. But the word of the Lord endureth for ever. Let us then build up all our hope upon this ever enduring word and upon the righteousness which it reveals. The Heavens shall vanish away like smoke. The Earth shall wax old as doth a garment & they that dwell therein shall die in like manner. But

God's salvation shall be for ever & this Righteousness shall never
be abolished. Let us therefore place all our hope in this righteousness & this salvation & we shall never be ashamed nor confounded
world without end. While I mention these things my heart is full
of affection to you and I hope you will consider what I have now
said as an expression of filial love & may the Lord give both you
and I understanding in all things.

With the warmest wishes of my heart for your and my
mother's happiness I ever am

My Dear Father

Most affectionately yours

David Dale

CHRONOLOGY OF MAIN EVENTS

1739   January 6th, Dale born in Stewarton.
1750's Apprentice in Paisley and agent in Cambuslang.
1763   Opening of shop in Hopkirk's Land in Glasgow.
1768   First Old Scotch Independents Meeting House erected in Greyfriars Wynd, Glasgow.
1769   Dale among the first elders (pastors) of the O.S.I.
1777   Marriage to Ann Caroline Campbell.
1778   Daughter (Anne Caroline) born.
1780   Dale buys land in Charlotte Street from Archibald Paterson.
1782   Partnership with Paterson dissolved.
1783   Moves to Charlotte Street.
        First Glasgow agent of the Royal Bank with Scott Moncrieff.
        Founder member of the Chamber of Commerce.
        Arkwright visits Glasgow.
        Death of youngest daughter from whooping-cough.
1785   First mill erected at New Lanark.
        Partnership with Arkwright severed.
        Enters into partnership with McIntosh (Turkey red at Dalmarnock).
1786   Spinning commences at New Lanark.
1787   Blantyre Mill established by Dale.
        Partnership with Alexander in Catrine Cotton Works.
        Made Director of Town's Hospital.
        Made full member of the Merchants' House.
        Chairman of the Chamber of Commerce.
1788   Fire at New Lanark.
1790   Director of the Glasgow Humane Society
1791   Spinningdale established.
        'Bailie Dale' chairs Town's Hospital Meeting.
        Involvement with Oban Mill ??
1792   Blantyre sold to James Monteith.
1795   Royal Infirmary opens. Dale one of the Managers.

1797   Owen's first visit to New Lanark.
1799   Owen buys New Lanark.
1800   Dale buys Rosebank.
1801   Catrine sold to James Finlay.
1804   Spinningdale sold.
1805   Dalmarnock sold to Henry Monteith.
1806   17th March, Dale dies at Rosebank.

Undated

Castle Douglas Mill.
Stanley Mill (between 1799–1806).
Partnership with Tennant & Todd in Barrowfield.
Death of infant son.

LIST OF ILLUSTRATIONS

BIBLIOGRAPHY

"Alfred" see under S. Kydd

Alison, R. *The Anecdotage of Glasgow*, Glasgow 1892.

Anderson, J.R., *Burgesses and Guild Brethren of Glasgow*, 2 vols. Scottish Record Society.

Annual Register 1792, London 1799.

Baines, E., *The History of the Cotton Manufacture in Great Britain*, London 1835.

Black, W.G., *David Dale's House*, Glasgow, Maclehose 1908.

Book of Glasgow Anecdotage, Glasgow 1912.

Bremner, D., *The Industries of Scotland*, Edinburgh, Black, 1869.

Brown, A., *The History of Glasgow*, Glasgow 1797.

Brown, J., *Religious Denominations of Glasgow*, 2 vols., Glasgow 1860.

Butt, J., (Ed.), *Robert Owen, Prince of Cotton Spinners*, David & Charles, Newton-Abbot 1971

Butt, J., *The Industrial Archaeology of Scotland*, David & Charles, Newton-Abbot 1967.

Calder, S.B., *The Industrial Archaeology of Scotland: A Scottish Highland Economy 1700–1900*, M. Litt., Strathclyde University 1974.

Chambers *Biographical Dictionary of Eminent Scotsmen*, London Blackie 1874.

Checkland, S.G., *Scottish Banking: A History 1695–1973*, Collins 1975.

Cleland, *Annals of Glasgow*, Glasgow 1817.

Cullen, A., *Adventures in Socialism*, Glasgow, J. Smith, 1910.

Dictionary of National Biography, O.U.P., 1888.

Extracts from the Records of the Burgh of Glasgow Vol III, 1781–95, Glasgow 1913.

Fitton, R.S. & Wadsworth, A.P., *The Strutts and the Arkwrights 1758–1830*, Manchester University Press 1958.

Fontana Economic History of Europe Vol. II, Collins 1974.

Garnett, T. *Observations on a Tour through the Highlands*, 2 vols. London 1800.

Glaister, J., *The Epidemic History of Glasgow 1783–1883*.

History of Lanark, A Guide to the Scenery, 3rd Edition, 1835.

Hume, J.R., *The Industrial Archaeology of Scotland*, Vol. 1, London, Batsford 1976.

"Income and Expenditure of the Town's Hospital 1796", Glasgow University Library Special Collection.

James Finlay & Co. Manufacturers & East India Merchants 1750–1950, Glasgow 1954.

Kydd, S. ("Alfred"), *The History of the Factory Movement from the Year 1802 to the Enactment of the Ten Hours Bill in 1847* 2 vols., London 1857.

Letters from Dale to Alexander, Mitchell Library, Glasgow MS 63.

Liddell, A., *Memoir of David Dale Esq.,* Glasgow 1854.

Maltby, S.E., *Manchester and the Movement for National Elementary Education 1800–1870,* Manchester 1918.

McNayr, J., *Guide from Glasgow to the Highlands of Scotland,* Glasgow 1797.

Mechie, S., *The Church and Scottish Social Development 1780–1870,* O.U.P. 1960.

Minutes of the Glasgow Humane Society, Glasgow 1790, in Strathclyde Regional Archives.

Munro, N., *The History of the Royal Bank of Scotland 1787–1927,* Edinburgh, Clark 1928.

Murray, D.B., *The Social and Religious Origins of Scottish Non-Presbyterian Dissent from 1730–1800,* Ph.D. Thesis, St Andrews 1976.

Murray, N., *Scottish Handloom Weavers 1790–1850: A Social History,* Edinburgh, J. Donald, 1978.

New Lanark Visitors' Book 1795–1799 in Glasgow University Archives.

New Statistical Account for Scotland, Edinburgh, Blackwood & Sons 1845.

Old Scotch Independent Church: General Register in Strathclyde Regional Archives.

Owen, R., *A New View of Society,* London 1813.

Owen, R., *The Life of Robert Owen by Himself,* Knight & Co., London 1971.

Owen, R., *Statement Regarding the New Lanark Establishment,* Edinburgh, J. Moir, 1812.

Regulations of the Town's Hospital with the Original Constitution of the House, Glasgow 1844.

R. Reid ("Senex"), *Glasgow Past & Present,* 3 vols. Glasgow 1844.

Reid, R., *Old Glasgow and its Environs,* Glasgow 1864;

Report of the Managers of the Royal Infirmary 1795, Mitchell Library.

Report of the Minutes of Evidence of the Select Committee on the State of Children Employed in the Manufactories of the U.K. Parliamentary Paper 1816.

Reports of the Society for Bettering the Condition and Increasing the Comforts of the Poor, 2 vols., London 1800.

Robertson, A.D., *Lanark, the Burgh and Its Councils 1469–1880.*

Royal Infirmary Charter 1792, Mitchell Library.

Senex: see under R. Reid.

Short Account of the Town's Hospital in Glasgow with the Abstracts of the Expenses for the First Three Years, 4th Edition, Edinburgh 1742.

Simon, B., (Ed.), *Education in Leicestershire 1540–1940,* Leicester University Press, 1968.

Sinclair, J., (Ed.), *The Old Statistical Account for Scotland,* 21 vols. Edinburgh 1790's.

Stanley, its History and Development, Dundee University Extra-Mural Department, 1977.

Stewart, G., *Curiosities of Glasgow Citizenship,* Glasgow, Maclehose 1881.

Substance of a Discourse by David Dale, 8th January 1792, Undated Publication in Glasgow University Library, Euing Collection.

Three Banks Review, No. 45, March 1960.

Town's Hospital Minutes 1732–1816, Mitchell Library MSS.

Worsdall, F., *The City that Disappeared,* Richard Drew, Glasgow 1981.

Join the Friends of New Lanark

The Friends of New Lanark is a voluntary association for people all over the world who are interested in the historic village, and who support the work of the New Lanark Conservation Trust.

By joining the Friends, you will receive various membership benefits - a quarterly newsletter, free admission to the New Lanark Visitor Centre, discounts in the Gift Shop and the New Lanark Mill Hotel.

Your subscription will also contribute to supporting a variety of projects each year which are of benefit to the village.

Contact the Friends at New Lanark Mills, Lanark ML11 9DB:
tel: 01555 667210 fax: 01555 665738 e-mail: friends@newlanark.org
or visit the New Lanark website: www.newlanark.org/friends/

He married
Dale's daughter.
He bought
Dale's mills.

Newtown raised him,
New Lanark
made him,
New Harmony
eluded him.

Robert Owen   **1771-1858**

From shop-boy to mill-owner,
from capitalist to socialist,
from autocrat to co-operator,

Discover Robert Owen at
The Robert Owen Museum
Broad Street, Newtown, Powys SY16 2BB

Open Monday to Friday and Saturday am.
Groups welcome. Phone 01686 626345

The David Livingstone Centre

Birthplace of Scotland's greatest Missionary and Explorer. Discover Livingstone's life from his childhood in the Blantyre Mills to his adventures in the heart of Africa. Museum housed in historic tenement built by David Dale in the 1780s.

Café and Gift Shop

Open All Year. Admission Charge.

Just off Junction 5 on the M74

Tel: Blantyre (01698) 823140

YOU KNOW US AS GROCERS

BUT WE'RE ALSO GROWERS

Everyone knows Co-op shops. But did you know that CWS, our parent organisation, is also Britain's biggest farmer? In fact, the CWS family of businesses spans a surprising range of sectors from finance to funerals, teabags to travel. What links all our businesses-like those of David Dale-is concern for community and adherence to a set of values focused on openness, honesty and social responsibility. For more information, visit the CWS website at www.co-op.co.uk or contact Scottish Co-op at: Robert Owen House, 87 Bath street, Glasgow G2 2EE (tel 0141 304 5400)

A family of businesses